P9-CNI-315

AMERICAN BUNGALOW STYLE

TEXT BY ROBERT WINTER

PHOTOGRAPHS BY ALEXANDER VERTIKOFF

An Archetype Press Book

Published in cooperation with *American Bungalow* magazine

SIMON & SCHUSTER

New York   London   Toronto   Sydney   Tokyo   Singapore

SIMON & SCHUSTER
Rockefeller Center
1230 Avenue of the Americas
New York, New York 10020

Printed in Hong Kong

10 9 8 7 6 5 4 3 2 1

Library of Congress Cataloging-in-Publication Data
Winter, Robert
American bungalow style / text by Robert Winter ; photographs
by Alexander Vertikoff
        p.   cm.
Includes bibliographical references and index.
1. Bungalows — United States — History. 2. Arts and crafts
movement — United States — Influence. I. Title.
NA7571.W557 1996
728′.373′0973 — dc20   95-39086

ISBN 0-684-80168-X (hardcover)

Endpapers and binding:
Honeysuckle wallpaper (1910)
reproduction (page 208). Courtesy
Bradbury and Bradbury.

Page 1: Milkcan lamp, a reproduction
of a Dirk Van Erp (1859–1933) copper
design with mica shades. Courtesy
Mica Lamps.

Page 2: A tall stone fireplace in
the den of an Altadena, California,
bungalow (pages 168–73)—the
heart of every home and a symbol
of the ideal family.

Part dividers. Pages 8–9: Morris Iris
wallpaper (1888, John Henry Dearle).
Courtesy Scalamandré. Pages 28–29:
Wallflower wallpaper (1890, Morris
and Company). Courtesy Scalamandré.
Pages 56–57: Thistle wallpaper (1900–
1920, English). Courtesy Bradbury and
Bradbury. Pages 194–95: Myrtle
wallpaper (1899, Morris and Company). Courtesy Scalamandré.

Produced by Archetype Press, Inc.,
Washington, D.C.
Project Director: Diane Maddex
Designer: Robert L. Wiser
Editorial Assistants: Gretchen Smith Mui,
Kristi Flis, and Christina Hamme

CONTENTS

FOREWORD

A small house, a large garden, a few friends, and many books.

—1910 bookplate inscription

Even the word has a friendly character: *bungalow.*

It bounces out of the mouth and rolls off the tongue in a pleasant, happy sort of way, one perfectly fitting the comfortable home that goes by that name. And recently the word has been happily bouncing out of the mouths of a whole new generation of Americans who have rediscovered the bungalow.

The phenomenon is not new. Years ago, in the early part of this century and through the 1920s and 1930s, America had a head-over-heels love affair with the simple, comfortable, and efficient house we call the bungalow.

Academics like to point out the bungalow's relationship to the Arts and Crafts movement—how the form found its way from India to England as a vacation home and then became an icon of the turn-of-the-century, liberal middle-class, American Arts and Crafts devotees who were seeking a rational answer to the excesses of the Victorian era and the dehumanizing machine-based lifestyle of the Industrial Age.

But the vast majority of the hundreds of thousands of bungalows that came to be built throughout North America were homes for people who had little philosophical attachment to the Arts and Crafts movement—if they knew of it at all. What popularized the bungalow was its basic honesty. As an American invention for individualists, it appealed to an awful lot of individual Americans. It was small and manageable, space efficient yet cozy. It was a do-it-yourself affair that did not require servants and often came with fruit trees and a vegetable garden to supply the family table. Simple Craftsman lines made the bungalow easy to build and maintain—and the style lent itself to precut kit houses that could be shipped anywhere near a railroad spur. The bungalow became the rage at a time when many Americans were moving from rented housing to their own homes. Bungalows popped up singly and in clusters all across the continent.

World War II changed everything, and the bungalow was no exception. In its place during the postwar building boom came the tract house, which was even easier to build. Skilled laborers were in short supply, and economy, not craftsmanship, was the strong suit of the ranch house. As America blossomed in the glow of victory, the bungalow fell into disfavor.

As essential as the fireplace in a bungalow was the front porch, from which the family could watch the world go by and take in the beauties of the garden. This Altadena, California, example (pages 64–69) provides an expansive view.

Millions of tract homes contributed to suburban sprawl, and shopping malls replaced the neighborhood market. The front porch disappeared. Back-yard patios and decks isolated people from their neighbors. The garage moved in with the family. Bungalow neighborhoods were now the "old" part of town, where only grandma still lived.

At each turn of the century, Americans have tended to indulge themselves in bouts of introspection and self-evaluation. Perhaps seeking some sort of closure, people examine the past to find their mistakes and look for those aspects of their lives that were worthwhile. The bungalow, along with the simple, self-sufficient life that it affords, is emerging a winner.

The most jaundiced, propaganda-bombarded generation the world has ever known is now finding satisfaction in real wood, stone, and brick—in the natural materials that are traditional in bungalows. Yet the fascination goes beyond nostalgia or mere interest in the house style. It is also a reaffirmation of genuineness and efficiency, as well as a concern for ecology. Bungalows can be cool in the summer and easy to heat in the winter. Often, they are conveniently close to downtown business areas. And each restored bungalow means one fewer tract house that will eventually end up in a landfill. The new bungalow movement also creates a commitment to community, because many of these homes can be found in big clusters of similar houses, with owners who share similar interests in creating rewarding places to live.

At *American Bungalow* magazine, we are privileged to hear daily from people across the country who tell us of adventures with their favorite bungalow, of the revitalization of whole neighborhoods, and of new construction embracing the bungalow philosophy. It is gratifying to assist in the movement, serving as a forum and "owner's manual" for those who have chosen a simpler, more artful style of life.

American Bungalow Style documents the bungalow in words and photographs as no other book has done. The author and photographer are old friends who have been with the magazine from the first issue and have encouraged, guided, assisted, and celebrated the new movement since its beginning. Whether you are an avid enthusiast or just discovering the world of the bungalow, this book is the perfect companion.

John Brinkmann
Publisher
American Bungalow magazine

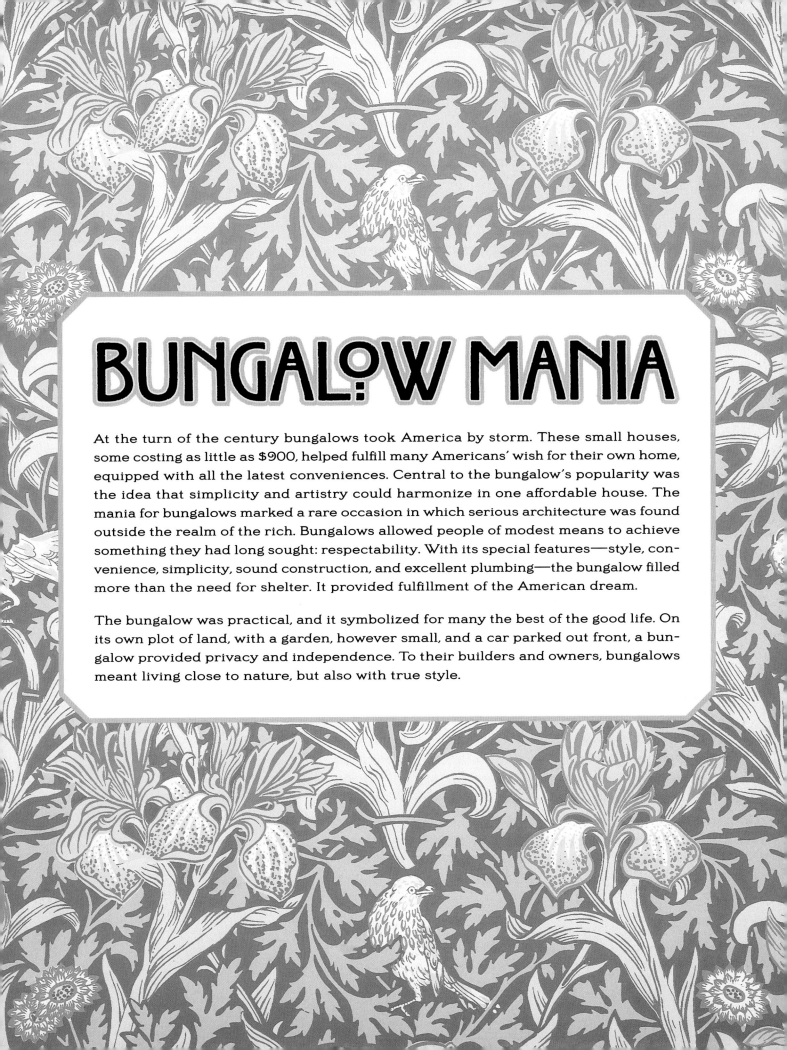

BUNGALOW MANIA

At the turn of the century bungalows took America by storm. These small houses, some costing as little as $900, helped fulfill many Americans' wish for their own home, equipped with all the latest conveniences. Central to the bungalow's popularity was the idea that simplicity and artistry could harmonize in one affordable house. The mania for bungalows marked a rare occasion in which serious architecture was found outside the realm of the rich. Bungalows allowed people of modest means to achieve something they had long sought: respectability. With its special features—style, convenience, simplicity, sound construction, and excellent plumbing—the bungalow filled more than the need for shelter. It provided fulfillment of the American dream.

The bungalow was practical, and it symbolized for many the best of the good life. On its own plot of land, with a garden, however small, and a car parked out front, a bungalow provided privacy and independence. To their builders and owners, bungalows meant living close to nature, but also with true style.

THE BUNGALOW DEFINED

What is a bungalow anyway? Where does the name come from? And what is so good about bungalows?

The definition seems easy. Most dictionaries are explicit: a bungalow is a one- or one-and-a-half-story dwelling. Good enough, except that since the period when most bungalows were produced—roughly 1880 to 1930 in the United States—literally every type of house has at one time or another been called a bungalow. Two-story houses built on the grounds of hotels are still called bungalows, for example. And to further muddy the matter, the great southern California architect Charles Sumner Greene went out of his way to call his Gamble house (1909) in Pasadena a bungalow (it is a spreading two-story residence with a third-floor pool room). Despite deviations in form, the dictionary definition of bungalows is the best point of departure. When bungalows were at their greatest popularity, most writers accepted this definition and usually apologized or tried to explain themselves when they departed from it.

A bungalow's chief distinction is its low profile. There are no vertical bungalows, even though in a few cities such as Sacramento, Seattle, and Vancouver, British Columbia, the basically horizontal house type is raised on high foundations. Promotional literature in the early twentieth century almost always noted that the chief purpose of the bungalow was to place most of the living spaces on one floor. The advantages are obvious: The absence of a second story simplifies the building process. Utilities can be installed more easily than in a two-story house. Safety is provided because, in case of fire, windows as well as doors provide easy escape. Best of all, the bungalow allows staircases to be eliminated, a boon for the elderly and also for the homemaker, who can carry out household tasks relieved of the stress created by stair climbing.

A common impression of the bungalow is that it must be small. To be sure, most bungalows are compact to save steps and filled with built-ins to conserve space (an aim that sometimes leads to claustrophobia). Many bungalows, however, are large—even very large—houses that preserve a horizontal line. Such commodious dwellings usually depended on the availability of cheap land: if the typical city lot could be augmented by extra land, the house could spread its wings—thus the relatively large bungalows in southern California and the mainly small ones cramped on narrow lots in the Chicago area.

Above: In the early years of the twentieth century Henry L. Wilson ("the bungalow man") helped spur the national craze for bungalows through *The Bungalow Magazine*. It was one of numerous magazines and books that spread the word about these compact and homey residences.

Opposite: More than a dozen bungalow ballads sang the praises of the Golden State's favorite new house type, particularly in the 1920s. The "Sunset Train" this song refers to is the Southern Pacific Railroad's "Sunset Limited," which traveled to New Orleans—far from "The Land of Flow'rs and Win-ter Show'rs."

In the Land of the Bungalow

"Just a little different"

bung'alo

Edw. F. Sweet Designing and Building Co.
Los Angeles, Cal.

THE WINDS OF DEMOCRACY

The answer to the question of where the term *bungalow* came from is not at all complicated. Throughout the period in which bungalow building flourished, authors of books and magazine articles traced the source to the Indian province of Bengal. There, the common native dwelling and the geographic area both had the same root word, *bangla* or *bangala.* Eighteenth-century huts of one story with thatched roofs were adapted by the British, who used them as houses for colonial administrators in summer retreats in the Himalayas and in compounds outside Indian cities. Also taking inspiration from the army tent, the English cottage, and sources as exotic as the Persian verandah, early bungalow designers clustered dining rooms, bedrooms, kitchens, and bathrooms around central living rooms and thereby created the essential floor plan of the bungalow, leaving only a few refinements to be worked out by later designers.

This house type spread to other parts of the British Empire and was copied by other turn-of-the-century imperial powers for use in their domains. The bungalow actually became a symbol of imperialism. The British, French, Dutch, and finally the Germans and Russians also domesticated bungalows by building them at home in seaside resorts, on lakefronts, and at mountain retreats. Eventually they built bungalows as suburban housing units and in working-class areas such as Paisley near Glasgow, Scotland.

Almost inevitably, this economical, practical type of house invaded North America, where it was well suited to the conditions of late-nineteenth- and early-twentieth-century population growth. Bungalows provided respectability and even style for émigrés to both country and city. The first American house actually referred to as a bungalow was designed in 1879 by William Gibbons Preston. Contrary to the usual definition, it was a two-story house built on Cape Cod at Monument Beach, Massachusetts, and was probably called a bungalow because it was in the tradition of resort architecture. A more orthodox bungalow was illustrated in 1884 in Arnold W. Brunner's *Cottages or Hints on Economical Building* as the frontispiece captioned "Bungalow (with attic)." This was a dormered Queen Anne–style cottage with an attic that was used for what Brunner called "dormitories." Otherwise the house generally conformed to the requirement that all main living quarters, including bedrooms, be located on the first floor.

From the East the idea moved westward. Naturally California—in everyone's mind the ultimate resort—was a promising locale for building bungalows. Land was relatively cheap, and the possibility of affordable and comfortable housing was attractive to the young on the make, the sick on the mend, and the old on modest pensions. The first California house designated as a bungalow was designed by the San Francisco architect A. Page Brown for J. D. Grant in the early 1890s. A true bungalow, this one-and-a-half-story residence was set on a high foundation and located on a hillside. It was a strange congeries of Bengalese, Queen Anne, and Swiss chalet architecture.

Above: Edward E. Sweet, a Los Angeles developer, used catalogues such as this one from about 1911 to sell bungalows to the public. The house, designed by Alfred Heineman, still stands in Pasadena, California.

Left: When this drawing was made in 1847, porches had already become important features of Himalayan "dak" bungalows. They were airy spots in which to escape hot Indian weather.

13

The bungalow craze actually took off after the turn of the century when Americans obsessed with the notion of health or simply attracted by the economic opportunity to be had in California began pouring into the state, a phenomenon that caused Charles Dudley Warner to speculate, "What sort of community will result from this union of the Invalid and the Speculator?" In the city of Los Angeles alone the population rose from 50,395 in 1890 to 1,238,048 in 1930. While other cities did not grow quite so fast, all but the northernmost part of the state participated in this phenomenal growth.

The demand for inexpensive but comfortable and even stylish housing advanced with the increase in population and, of course, contributed dramatically to the popularity of the bungalow. Its success in California was paralleled in the rest of the United States, where developers and construction companies often identified the house type with the Golden State, calling it "the California bungalow." Although the first bungalows were created in the East, the idea was exploited in the American West and then moved eastward again. As the historian Frederick Jackson Turner said, in a somewhat different context, "The winds of democracy blow east." The building of bungalows became a national phenomenon in every part of the country that encountered population growth in the 1910s and 1920s—just about everywhere.

Before World War I a small bungalow could be built for $900, according to the not-always-accurate sales pitches of the time. A good-sized bungalow might cost $3,500. Considering that even $900 was then quite an outlay for a family of modest means, the bungalow was not built by the poor or even the lower middle classes, but it was affordable for people with steady jobs. Even when prices took off in the 1920s, would-be homeowners with average incomes could afford to construct or buy a bungalow, although, because of high interest rates on mortgages, some were ruined in economic downturns such as the Great Depression of the 1930s.

Ironically, the house type that had once been the symbol of retreat to the countryside became the architecture of the city and its suburbs. Yet the bungalow did not lose its identification with the rural idyll and a better, golden day. Be it ever so humble, it embodied an ideal for the majority of Americans—the freestanding, single-family dwelling set down in a garden, an ideal that clings to us today, especially as that goal seems threatened by a more complex and certainly much more populous society.

About 1920 Mr. and Mrs. Isaac Tolman Judson and their family posed proudly in front of their bungalow in Orland, California. Secure behind a rubblestone wall and sheltered by swooping gables, the bungalow proclaimed its respectability.

SELLING THE BUNGALOW

Something more than its practicality coupled with the dream of Eden (California) sold the bungalow to Americans. An excitement about it was stirred by the popular press and magazines, many of them directed at women who were traditionally devoted to domestic concerns. *Good Housekeeping, House Beautiful, Ladies' Home Journal,* and many other women's magazines adopted the bungalow as a cause. The real estate sections of newspapers carried articles almost every week on "particularly interesting" bungalows, for men were also attracted to them. Henry L. Wilson, who advertised himself as "the bungalow man," established a journal devoted to the subject, *The Bungalow Magazine,* published first in Los Angeles, then Seattle, and finally Chicago. Even the professional architecture journals, which might be expected to be suspicious of the homely cottage, could not ignore it. In fact, some of the best articles on the bungalow can be found in professional journals such as *Architectural Forum* and *Architectural Record* in the years before World War I.

Opposite: Although the bungalow is usually associated with the Arts and Crafts movement before World War I, its greatest popularity came in the 1920s. During that decade revivals of historic architectural styles—from English cottages to Spanish haciendas—were in vogue, spurred on by plan books such as this one.

Below: Canny business people exploited the bungalow to promote sales of their own products. In this case, the tomatoes may have had more character than the house.

BUNGALOW

SHIPPED BY
E.K.SAKAI & Co.
TOPPENISH, WASHINGTON.

At least in the period from 1900 to 1920, the bungalow was closely associated with the Arts and Crafts movement, which had been founded in England in the late 1880s as a clarion call for unity of design, humanization of labor, and quality for everyone. One of the movement's founders, William Morris (1834–96)—a devout reformer who could never seem to produce anything that the common person could afford—would have been delighted with the American bungalow. In spite of his apparent radicalism, he was a sentimental Marxist who really wanted to return to a preindustrial handicraft society. It is an understatement to say that Morris's socialism never caught on in America, but his sentimentality certainly did. On the minds of many Americans, including some industrialists, was the concern that industrialism, however successful in some ways, had turned into a disappointment, alienating people from the products of their work, breaking up families, causing depression, and even driving people into crime. It is in this way that Morris's ideas were interpreted in America.

The almost-too-perfect leader of the American Arts and Crafts movement was Gustav Stickley (1858–1942), the founder and editor of *The Craftsman* magazine, which was the chief organ for American Arts and Crafts ideas. At the same time Stickley was a businessman who in his own factory near Syracuse, New York, turned out beautifully crafted furniture by employing machines as well as workers. If this description suggests that he compromised with industrialism, so he did. What he wanted to do, like his contemporary, Theodore Roosevelt, was reform industry rather than abolish it, to soften the effect of the machine by putting it to use in bettering human lives.

It is no wonder that in *The Craftsman* (1901–16) Stickley crusaded for bungalows that would give the working class as much respectability as business people attained from their mansions. Here, in the simple dwelling set in a garden, was a symbol of preindustrial individualism. In a sense, it humanized cities by allowing workers all the best aspects of rural living and at the same time all the blessings of an urban civilization. *The Craftsman* probably did more than any other magazine to further the idea of the bungalow in the United States. Stickley even built a bungalow for himself near Morris Plains, New Jersey (pages 88–93), and filled it not only with furniture from his United Crafts factory (renamed Craftsman Workshops in 1904) but also with Grueby ceramics and other Arts and Crafts products.

Magazines were not the only promotional literature available on bungalows. Several books were written on the subject. Of these, the most important were *Bungalows* (1911) by Henry H. Saylor and *The Bungalow Book* (1923) by Charles E. White, Jr., published at the height of bungalow construction. Saylor's book, which came out in the period of the "high art"

Above: A Morris chair in front of a tiled fireplace, cozy window seats on either side—this was the bungalow vision encouraged by *The Craftsman* in 1905. Below: In another issue of the magazine, a brick hearth warmed a "bachelor's bungalow."

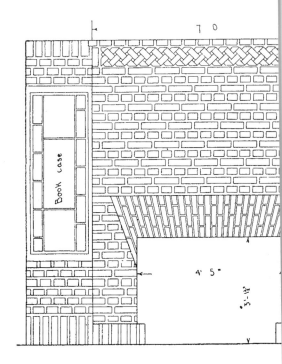

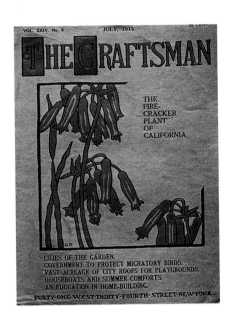

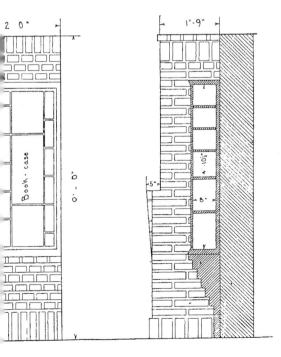

Above: Gustav Stickley's magazine, *The Craftsman,* was a great champion of the bungalow. Its covers from around 1913 were designed in a high style that common bungalows rarely attained, but the two were related in their homey type of realism.

bungalow and the Arts and Crafts era, was nicely divided into chapters with such titles as "Types," "The Plan," "Roof Materials," "Furniture and Furnishings," "Fireplaces," "Lighting Systems," "Sewage Disposal," and even "Planting." It mainly gave practical advice on its subjects and thus is a rich resource for present-day restorers. White's book is similar except that, being an architect (in the Prairie School), he is more thorough on topics such as construction and details such as dumbwaiters, door mats, telephones, electrical gadgets, and garages. Readers of these books would have had no trouble knowing what to look for in the ideal bungalow. Hundreds of other smaller books also gave tips on good design. William Phillips Comstock's *Bungalows, Camps and Mountain Houses* (1908, 1915, 1924, with Clarence Eaton Schermerhorn) dispenses plenty of advice, the 1924 edition even containing a section on bungalows in Puerto Rico and other territories in "the American tropics."

The greatest stimulus for the spread of bungalows throughout the United States was business enterprise. Literally hundreds of books, some in hard cover but most of them in rather solid but smaller pamphlets, were produced by salespeople eager to profit from bungalow mania. They showed elevations and floor plans and then encouraged potential customers to write for detailed drawings so that the local carpenter could construct every detail with complete confidence. In *The Bungalow Book* (1910) Henry L. Wilson advertised his desire to deliver a complete set of plans consisting of "a foundation and cellar plan, floor plans, four elevations and all necessary details and a complete set of specifications" for only $10 and also estimated the cost of construction, which was usually under $3,000. Most of the writers of these books and pamphlets warned their readers of the dire consequences of having their carpenter build their house without complete plans, but it is safe to say that many bungalows were put up based on only one elevation and one floor plan.

The Southern California Standard Building Company not only produced its own bungalow book enticing prospective customers with dreams of good design but also sold real estate and arranged for loans and insurance. For people who lived in the East, Standard would even take over their property and give them "something in Sunny California" in exchange. Noting its comprehensive package, Standard stood by its slogan, "We Can Do It."

The success of the bungalow led its designers and promoters to change its original purpose. At first one of the beauties of the bungalow was that it gave the average person an opportunity to live in a single-family, one-story house with a garden. What happened when efficiency-minded developers chose to make even more economical use of the land? The answer in Chicago was to build narrow bungalows that covered most of the narrow city lots and thus eliminated all but a tiny garden. An approach to the same problem in California and elsewhere was the "double bungalow," a semidetached structure that preserved some of the garden at the expense of the idea of a freestanding house. The designs were often ingenious and sometimes good looking, but privacy was compromised by higher density.

BUNGALOW COURTS

California came up with another answer to the problem of density: the bungalow court. In 1909 Sylvanus Marston, a young architect educated at Cornell's school of architecture, was commissioned by a developer to design a group of bungalows in Pasadena. They were to be assembled around a modest court and, although relatively small, provide wealthy visitors to California a place in the sun, far from the rigors of eastern winters. St. Francis Court, as it was called, provided them with all the amenities from Persian rugs and up-to-date kitchens to rooms for servants. It was a successful—albeit upper-class—speculation that gave rise to more plebeian efforts. Also in Pasadena, Bowen Court (1911), designed by the firm of Arthur S. Heineman with Alfred Heineman serving as project architect, was much more modest in its intentions and had a greater concentration of bungalows—and people. Twenty-three tiny bungalows were constructed on a large L-shaped lot. The great Arts and Crafts architect Charles Sumner Greene was aghast at this clever speculative device: "It would seem," he wrote, "to have no other reason for being than that of making money for the investor." And he added, "This is a good example of what not to do."

The bungalow court idea was greatly exploited not only in California but also in the rest of the United States and Canada, not as resort architecture but as housing for people of modest means. It was, in a sense, an alternative to the apartment houses that were appearing in cities in the 1920s. The bungalow was used also for hotels. The Heineman firm was responsible for building grouped houses where motorists might spend the night and was apparently the first to call the grouping a "mo-tel."

Above: With its beamed ceiling and arched brick fireplace, a living room in Sylvanus Marston's St. Francis Court showed great flair. Right: Simpler bungalows populated the later Bowen Court, which centered on a rustic clubhouse.

ALADDIN
HOMES

Manufactured by
the ALADDIN
COMPANY

Bay City
Michigan

MAIL-ORDER BUNGALOWS

Another important refinement of business strategy was the prefabricated or "ready-cut" bungalow, whose parts were mass-produced in a factory, numbered, loaded on a freight car, and then sent to any part of the country where a skilled carpenter could put them together "in a day" by following the complete specifications provided. Probably the most famous of these mail-order firms was Sears, Roebuck and Company, but in the 1910s and 1920s a number of others throughout the United States and Canada also advertised their ability to provide prefabricated bungalows. The most important of these was the Aladdin Company, based in Bay City, Michigan, with plants in Hattiesburg, Mississippi; Wilmington, North Carolina; and Portland, Oregon. Aladdin drew on the popular association of the bungalow with California in designs named The Pomona, The Pasadena, The Burbank, and The Sunshine. Other names evoked the bungalow's ability to survive in colder climes—The Genesee, The Plymouth, The Kentucky, joined by The Tacoma, The Willamette, and The Spokane.

Advertising that it operated on "The Golden Rule" (a motto its public relations people boasted was backed by a U.S. patent), Aladdin was so proud of the quality of its product that it offered customers one dollar for every knot they could find in the wooden components. Because of the company's efficiencies, Aladdin asserted that it could sell its house kits for around $1,000, well below the price of a custom-built bungalow. Conscious of middle-class Americans' desire for well-built houses at low cost, the company noted that it had created a "Board of Seven," a design team that scrutinized every phase of production. Aladdin observed that "unless the cost of these high-priced men's time could be spread over a hundred or more houses of each design, the cost would be prohibitive. But when they spend two hours or more hours valuable time on the design, drawings and cutting sheets of an Aladdin house, the cost is not all charged to that *one house* but to *several hundred* houses of that *same design* sold during the year." Around 1920 rows of Aladdin bungalows sprang up in Roanoke Rapids, North Carolina (page 43), one of a number of company towns built or expanded quickly with mail-order residences.

In Bay City, Michigan, Aladdin was joined by another "ready-cut" house company. The Lewis Manufacturing Company produced bungalows similar in style and interior arrangement to those of Aladdin. So did Harris Brothers of Chicago and Gordon–Van Tine of Davenport, Iowa, as well as Sears, Montgomery Ward, and Pacific Ready-Cut in Los Angeles. At least one factory was located in Vancouver, British Columbia. These mail-order firms manufactured bungalows that were humble, but with their intelligent floor plans, built-ins, and fireplaces they were as respectable as any larger house built nearby.

Above: Aladdin's Pasadena-model bungalow was promoted in the company's 1919 mail-order catalogue with a perspective plan of the house. Little was left to the imagination in terms of visualizing its possibilities, down to a Victrola phonograph in the corner of the living room.

Opposite: The catalogue endpaper, showing the exterior of the Pasadena, evoked the refinement of Little Lord Fauntleroy that the bungalow was expected to provide.

BUNGALOW BUILDERS

All the major architects of the time—from Bernard Maybeck and Frank Lloyd Wright to Charles and Henry Greene—as well as most of the less noted ones, designed bungalows. The great majority of bungalows, however, came from people who were never identified in print. Developers and construction firms often hired young architects who had not yet established practices on their own. The Pasadena construction company of Austin and Grable, for example, produced some beautiful bungalows, leading one authority to conclude that the Austin of the firm was the well-known Los Angeles architect John C. Austin; it has been established, however, that he had nothing to do with the firm. The real designer was banished to anonymity.

And who were the designers of prefabricated and pattern-book bungalows? In the manner of big business, the faces of the creative people usually faded into the process of industry. Exceptions can be found. Early in the century writers of how-to-do-it books such as Henry L. Wilson and Charles E. White, Jr., and a few salespeople such as William Phillips Comstock were at pains to credit the designers of the bungalows they presented. But in most bungalow books and pamphlets, finding the architect of a particular house is usually a chance discovery.

Alfred Heineman designed a number of bungalows for his brother Arthur's architectural firm but sometimes sold design rights to promoters. Around 1911 one of his bungalows appeared on the cover of a little brochure entitled *Sweet's Bungalows* (pages 12–13), and several exteriors and interiors of his buildings were illustrated in it. A picture of his Bowen Court in Pasadena (pages 20–21) appeared on the cover of Clyde J. Cheney's *Artistic Bungalows* (1912). The Heineman firm was not even mentioned in either book. Another designer employed by Cheney was Ross Montgomery, but the only way one would know that is because Montgomery signed his handsome rendering "RM del" (delineator). Only knowledge of his style from other signed designs allows identification. It is possible that Montgomery may have been the artist who touched up an interior view that Cheney plagiarized from Gustav Stickley's *The Craftsman* (page 18).

Below: Ross Montgomery gave himself a quiet credit for one of his house designs. Right: Lawrence Fournier designed his 1910 Minneapolis house (pages 94–99) before he became a skilled draftsman in the office of Purcell, Feick and Elmslie.

BUNGALOWS REDUX

At the same time that the bungalow was being altered for higher-density living in bungalow courts and mail-order houses, it somehow lost its glamour. The spirit seemed drained from its proponents. Bungalows had always been disparaged by those who equated a high standard of living with the two-story house. The prosperity of the 1920s also had something to do with the loss in esteem for the modest house. The waning of the Arts and Crafts movement led to the stage scenery of period revival buildings. In these circumstances the little house was set aside or laughed at—a fact that gave meaning to Woodrow Wilson's epithet for his arch-enemy, Henry Cabot Lodge: "bungalow minded."

Then came the stock market crash of 1929, followed by the Great Depression in the 1930s. The hard times were very hard on the idea of architecture for people of modest means. After World War II bungalow building revived, but the new houses went under new names such as the Cape Cod cottage, the ranch house, and the tract home. The term *bungalow* was used to disparage the small house built earlier in the century. Until fairly recently it thus was possible for developers of condominiums and freeways to plow through bungalowlands everywhere without much thought or public condemnation.

The last ten years have seen a revival of interest in the bungalow. People are moving back to the old bungalow neighborhoods that still exist and calling them "bungalow heavens." In fact, the bungalow—like its predecessor, the Victorian house—is becoming gentrified. Several books and many articles have been written on the subject, and a magazine, *American Bungalow*, has been created to reflect and encourage the revival of the bungalow. On whole streets and blocks, pleasant but aesthetically undistinguished cottages have been preserved and a spirit of community prevails—or has been recreated. The modesty and even conventionality of the housing masks the fact that these neighborhoods often have a high degree of social cohesion, in which neighbor looks out for neighbor and where restrictions are self-imposed by the residents. Our age craves the restoration of the family and even the respectability that the bungalow once provided.

Above: Chicago is one of the many American cities that have retained entire bungalow neighborhoods. Its examples, like these two, date mostly from the 1920s. Brick was the material of choice and was often brightened with shimmering art glass.

Opposite: This geometric facade design was influenced by Art Deco ideas, which were merged with the earlier Arts and Crafts movement.

BUNGALOW STYLE

With its cozy fireplace inside and its bucolic garden outside, few turn-of-the-century house types embodied the idea of home better than the bungalow. They came in a variety of architectural styles, but what did they have in common?

Bungalows were generally freestanding, single-family houses, small according to the standards of the period. They were practical, one- or one-and-a-half-story dwellings with few or no stairs to climb. Economical to build, bungalows were generally crafted simply but well. They were usually sited on flat land and were normally visible from the street. Most had front porches, patios, or, as in Chicago, sunrooms with bands of windows so that the street was clearly visible. Through their smallness, they helped keep the family together—the conscious embodiment of the American dream. Bungalows expressed a nostalgia for the past in a multitude of popular historic architectural styles, recalling the ideals of simpler times and creating neighborhoods where the best aspects of democracy are alive and functioning even today.

ARCHITECTURAL STYLES

Architecture is much more than style, but an important factor in the construction of bungalows was their ability to meet owners' functional requirements while giving them what had previously been limited to the wealthy few: the latest designs. High-style bungalows were created by Frank Lloyd Wright, Bernard Maybeck, William Gray Purcell, and other notable American architects. Most bungalows were not high art, however. The humbler types were what people of moderate means could afford.

Bungalows reflected the whole range of architectural movements of their day, from Queen Anne to Arts and Crafts, Tudor to Prairie and Pueblo, Spanish to English Colonial Revival, and even Moderne. One of the first styles used for bungalows—then often called cottages—was Queen Anne, a name given to English country houses whose classical details were applied to basically medieval forms. The style's eclecticism garnered great popularity among would-be country squires, but it also became associated with late-nineteenth-century English cities—red brick structures with high-pitched roofs and prominent chimneys.

In the United States the bungalow craze started in southern California before it spread to nearly every American town. California's climate was perfect for bungalows and for the Arts and Crafts styles in particular. These styles—California, Prairie, Mission, and Tudor—have in common a conscious search for the supposed simplicity of preindustrial times. All versions were meant to counter the excesses of the Victorian period by returning to a preindustrial past when handicrafts displayed personal involvement in the products of a laborer's work. While interested mainly in the creation of accessories for the home, Arts and Crafts designers also searched for an architecture that would return to honesty and be emblematic of an era, usually the Middle Ages, when an organic society inspired an organic architecture.

Although mostly looking backward to an allegedly better day, the styles were never really medieval but Tudor at the earliest and neoclassical at the latest. It is easy to see how the bungalow, whose existence was defended on the grounds of restoring family values, fit beautifully into the Arts and Crafts movement. It would bring style to all people whatever their economic or social status, a fundamental goal of the followers of William Morris, the founder and saint of the Arts and Crafts movement in Britain.

As the following survey indicates, later period revivals that sought different pasts— Native American, Spanish, early American—also captured the hearts of bungalow lovers during the house's heyday from 1880 to 1930. Some of the styles developed before 1880, of course, and lasted beyond 1930, but they endure today in thousands of fine remaining bungalows.

"Five rooms, neat porch," proclaimed Sears, Roebuck when it introduced its Crescent mail-order bungalow in 1921. With its gabled portico and grouped columns, the house recalled America's early Georgian-style buildings. This one, with an optional two extra upstairs rooms, arrived in Washington, D.C., in 1926.

Queen Anne (1885–1905)

In the United States the Queen Anne style's silhouette became asymmetrical, picturesque, and somewhat rambling. It contrasted materials and colors and featured wraparound porches, balconies, and highly decorative materials from sculptured brick chimneys to art glass windows. Queen Anne cottages or bungalows sprang up in the East in the late 1880s and quickly spread to California, where they became identified with the state's lifestyle.

Although the English country house was faced with red bricks or tiles, the American Queen Anne bungalow was typically clad in clapboards or shingles. Like English cottages, it had a medium-pitched roof that sometimes sprouted one or two dormer windows, betraying the fact that the attic—the half story of the one-and-a-half-story bungalow—was used for living spaces. At least one porch with a little jigsaw ornament (gingerbread) around its openings was required.

The interiors were typical Victorian rooms, except that the usual living room and parlor were merged into one room. Wallpapered walls were interrupted by a picture molding a foot or so below the ceiling. Occasionally a corner tower gave distinction to the living room.

California Style (1900–1930)

In its day the term *California bungalow* evoked both a type—a one- or one-and-a-half-story dwelling—and an Arts and Crafts architectural style that merged elements from Japanese buildings and Swiss chalets. The type and the style were confused in the period of bungalow building and continue to cause confusion. The grand houses of the Pasadena architects Charles and Henry Greene embody the California style, but, at a full two stories, they do not fit the type's dictionary definition. And in spite of a common assumption to the contrary, the brothers Greene were not the inventors of the style (or the type) but were simply highly skilled practitioners of a well-worn tradition.

California-style bungalows always have street-facing gables with composition or shingled roofs. To merge with nature they are usually painted or stained brown or dark green. Their eaves are wide and hovering.

The front door usually opens directly into the living room. There, a strong predilection for wood is expressed in dark paneling. The ceiling is usually plastered, and wooden beams may cross it in geometric patterns. From the living room to the dining room and den, the tone is dark and wooden, finished with a light but dull varnish.

There is always a fireplace, a symbol of home. It may be of brick, stone, cobblestone, or tile, but it must be present, preferably in an inglenook. Casement windows, sometimes containing art glass, bring in some light, but shadows prevail. Usually an arched opening flanked by bookcases separates the living room from the dining room, which is also paneled—and dark. A built-in sideboard is almost mandatory.

Beyond, the bungalow takes on a different mood. Bedrooms are light, with woodwork painted white or another light color. Often wallpaper is used to cheer the hearts of those who may have been put off by the gloom of the front rooms. Arts and Crafts proponents frowned on bright, highly patterned paper because it contrasted with art objects, but no such objection was made to wallpaper in the back rooms. The bathroom (usually there is only one) is also white to signify cleanliness, and so is the kitchen, with its panoply of gadgets and many built-ins that save space.

Opposite: Wooden wainscoting in California-style bungalows often rises to within a foot of the ceiling, leaving a frieze to be filled with grass cloth, wallpaper, stenciling, or pictures.

Mission Style (1890–1915)

The Mission phenomenon of the Arts and Crafts movement was not limited to California, Florida, and the Southwest, but it was used most often in states with a Spanish past. Although the late Queen Anne, called the Shingle Style, looked back to America's colonial Northeast, Mission style drew on Hispanic church architecture. Its message, even in humble bungalows, was antimachine, antimodern.

Key identifying characteristics are tile roofs, vaguely Moorish towers, and round arches recalling a mission cloister. Inside, the rooms are usually plain, functional spaces whose main interest comes from fireplaces and perhaps a little art glass. Applied to bungalows, the style dictates austerity, although sometimes humorous attempts were made to transcend the Spartan aesthetic.

Opposite: In the Tomek house (1907) in Riverside, Illinois, a Prairie Style bungalow, Frank Lloyd Wright made one of his assertive brick fireplaces the core of the home. The horizontal lines of narrow Roman bricks help recall Wright's beloved prairie. A straight and simple mantel continues the horizontal theme, while bands of wood give the small house a sense of flowing space.

Tudor Style (1890–1930)

In the late nineteenth century the American architectural scene experienced a Colonial Revival, both Anglo and Spanish. The Tudor style is an allusion to the architecture of the mother country of the Puritans and an era before the machine took over.

The most conspicuous trait of Tudor exteriors is its black-and-white work, in which wooden beams, supposedly blackened by time, pose against white plaster or stucco. This sort of display was merely decorative—just as in the sixteenth century—but it was emblematic of the Arts and Crafts goal of expressing structural honesty.

Casement windows often were diamond-paned, which produced a closed-in, homey touch. The interior arrangement was precisely the same as in the California and Prairie Style bungalows, with paneling up to a plate rail a foot or so from the ceiling, thus giving room for a frieze. Rarely was an attempt made to apply Tudor ornament, even on the fireplace, where it might be expected.

Exposed beams and plaster facades also characterized a 1920s Tudor spinoff, the Norman or French Provincial style. Their interiors rarely displayed recognizably French features, and few attempts were made to articulate furnishings and style.

Prairie Style (1900–1920)

At the time the California style was developing, Frank Lloyd Wright was producing a related but different style in the Midwest. What Wright and others had in mind was an architecture that expressed horizontality in much the way that the California bungalow did—buildings set on foundations close to the ground, with low-pitched roofs and wide eaves.

In about 1901 Wright inaugurated a series of Prairie Style houses. Strongly influenced by the linearity of Japanese prints, he created a recognizably new style with rows of casement windows, low chimneys, and asymmetrically placed entrances that often are almost hidden from view; porches, walls, and terraces further extended the houses into the landscape.

A wide group of devotees was attracted to his ideas, particularly a flat-roofed, concrete design in the April 1907 issue of the *Ladies' Home Journal* entitled "A Fireproof House for $5,000." Bungalow builders picked up on this addition to their Arts and Crafts portfolios, even though—limited by the bungalow's small size—they could not develop Wright's famous flowing spaces inside. They also rarely had a chance to design the furnishings, as Wright did in his organic, fully coordinated houses.

Period Revivals (1915–30)

Period revival styles—such as Spanish, pueblo, log, and colonial—are usually thought of as projections of the 1920s, but each had its roots in the recent as well as the distant past. The Spanish Colonial Revival, for example, took off from the Mission style but found its inspiration in Spanish haciendas as well as churches. The popular Panama-California International Exposition, held in San Diego in 1915, took a new look at America's Spanish heritage. The fair, supervised by the distinguished architect Bertram Grosvenor Goodhue, created a new wave of Hispanic interest throughout the United States.

Rural structures such as English (Cotswold) cottages, French chateaux, and New England farmhouses (Cape Cod cottages) were other popular models for period revival styles.

Rather than picking out one or several preferred features, as in the Queen Anne style, period house designers attempted to suggest accurate massing, proportions, materials, and details of earlier buildings. The eclecticism of previous revivals was dropped in favor of authentic recastings of historic styles. Interiors reflected newly informal lifestyles with more open plans and flowing spaces.

Spanish Colonial Revival (1915–30)

Building on interest in America's missions, a number of architects went beyond the Hispanic architecture in the United States to draw imagery from Mexico and Spain itself, especially from domestic architecture. In doing so, they opened a new architectural vocabulary, called Plateresque and Churrigueresque.

The high art of Bertram Goodhue and others had to be watered down in its application to the bungalow. Not many baroque doorways appeared on these small houses. The better-than-average Spanish Colonial Revival bungalow, however, did have some endearing ornaments. Canvas draperies that could be pulled across large, round-arched windows were fairly common features, as were awnings supported by spears over doorways. And, of course, there was always a red tile roof.

Interiors were bathed with light, thanks to large windows and white or rosy pink walls, against which almost any style of furniture looked good. Black iron balustrades and curtain rods were used, with curtains hung on wooden rings. Much tile, either Mexican or American, appeared on staircases and in bathrooms and kitchens. Although a Spanish fireplace was set in the corner of the living room, references to Spain occurred mainly outside.

Pueblo Revival (1915–30)

The Pueblo Revival style is closely related to the Spanish Colonial Revival. In a sense, it is part of a search for a truly American style that is behind all the revivals of the 1920s. If Spanish haciendas or Tudor cottages were not satisfactory models, then what about the architecture of the Native American?

The result was a building that looked as if it were made of adobe bricks but that in fact was conventional wooden, balloon-frame construction covered with stucco. More elaborate versions of this style included vigas, the ends of the poles that supported second floors and roofs of seventeenth-century Spanish and American Indian buildings in the Southwest. Flat roofs were in vogue, some of them stepped back in true pueblo style. Even a ladder might be tilted against the wall. Rounded corners and rough surfaces mimicked the feel of hand-applied adobe. Rough wooden window lintels and porch posts could have been logged in nearby forests. And if bougainvillea was not actually present, it was a part of the psychic scene.

The Native American theme was carried inside by using Navajo rugs and other Indian artifacts. Sometimes Indian bowls became lampshades, but this was rare.

Log Cabin Revival (1915–30)

Those who believed that the Cape Cod cottage was a somewhat superficial style could turn to the rude architecture of the frontier for something that was truly indigenous (even though it has since been proved that the log cabin was introduced to America by the Swedes and Finns). The resonance was a nostalgia not simply for Daniel Boone but also for a preindustrial America when family virtues were exhibited in plain yet sturdy dwellings.

The revival of log cabins coexisted with the rise of rustic lodges and distinctive national park architecture ("Parkitecture"), both outgrowths of the Arts and Crafts movement, both expressing a need to get back to nature. In the Adirondacks, wealthy weekenders built "camps" for themselves that resembled giant Swiss chalets erected log by log. Similar designs appeared in hotels and other rural retreats designed to lure city dwellers out to the countryside.

Log cabin bungalows, however, are extremely rare but are fun to watch for. Even Gustav Stickley, the chief protagonist of Arts and Crafts ideas in the United States, used logs for his Craftsman Farms in New Jersey (pages 88–93) to make sure that his own bungalow appeared to commune properly with nature.

Colonial Revival (1915–30)

At the turn of the century the Ecole des Beaux-Arts in Paris sent the message that architecture is essentially bilateral symmetry and that style must be classically inspired. Translated into the language of bungalow designers, this meant the design of miniature temple fronts or, more often, the use of Georgian or Federal-style models from the eighteenth century, which produced the Colonial Revival.

Little effort was made to enforce the Colonial Revival on interiors except to paint woodwork white. Books by interior designers suggested that Arts and Crafts furniture by Stickley and others also be painted white. The enormous popularity of the Colonial Revival resulted in many Arts and Crafts bungalows becoming white inside and out. The Cape Cod cottage (sometimes known as the "Cape Coddage") extended this style into the 1930s and 1940s.

A spinoff was a boxy bungalow, common in bungalow tracts, that *The Craftsman* called "The Urban House." The exterior is usually exceedingly plain, with perhaps a dash of classical detail. Its chief stylistic feature is a grouping of windows in bands. The interiors are flooded with light from these windows and french doors that lead to front porches or patios.

Moderne (1930–40)

Art Deco may have been too high style to be used for the modest bungalow, but in the 1930s quite a few bungalows were designed in what is now called Streamline Moderne.

Outside, they were characterized by curved corners, inspired by newly streamlined locomotives and engineering feats such as "Airflow" Chryslers. The Cunard Line's *Queen Mary* was also a source of portholes, bulkheads, and other "up-to-date"— modern—features. Concrete and stucco, often in pastel hues, were common building materials. Glass brick was used, especially around entrances. Terra-cotta ornament provided accents. When windows continued around corners, they underscored the sense of motion inherent in the style.

Bungalow interiors were rarely outstanding examples of the Moderne style, which was usually saved for more expensive buildings. But they were light and airy and might even have some modernistic furniture, which at the time was not expensive. Some pieces were stepped back like modern skyscrapers or zigzagged to capture the energy of electricity and the Jazz Age. Steel, chrome, and aluminum entered the modern age, and Venetian blinds closed it out.

THE GARDEN

The ideal bungalow was surrounded by a garden, however small. Garden plans usually were based on the occupants' needs and desires, but some more sophisticated plans came from the hands of landscape architects. As with other gardens, bungalow landscapes were either formal or informal, with the informal ones most often being Japanese.

The typical California bungalow, wherever it was found, was set back from the street to allow at least a small lawn. Shrubbery would be planted close to the facade. In California a palm tree somewhere on the property, near the house, was expected. In eastern cities where land was relatively expensive, such as Chicago and Brooklyn, the lot would be narrow, around thirty feet wide. As a result, there was little if any lawn in front so that as much house as possible could sit on the property. Front landscaping would usually be confined to the parkway between the street and the sidewalk in eastern city bungalow tracts. In the 1920s, when land prices in the West began to rise and lawns diminished, the parkway was simi larly the chief landscaped area; in southern California palm trees often appeared here also.

A yard in back was a necessary appurtenance of bungalows everywhere. In the East and Midwest it was rather small, with a little room for a vegetable patch and perhaps a croquet lawn. In the West, particularly on larger lots in California, it could be given more elaborate treatment.

Many gardening books were published in the period from 1900 to 1930, but few were directed explicitly at what should be done on a small scale. The only treatise on bungalow gardens is a little book by Eugene O. Murmann entitled *California Gardens* (1914). In spite of its obvious regional emphasis, it was, as Murmann himself suggests, aimed at a national audience. He argued that by substituting a few plants and trees for those that grow only in a semitropical environment, one could use the book's photographs and plans. For a few dollars Murmann would, moreover, help bungalow owners select the proper plants and provide them with a plan showing exactly where they should go.

Many ideas can be taken from Murmann's folksy wisdom and used in any part of the country. Unfortunately, without Murmann's business records, it is not known how popular his ideas were.

In *The Bungalow Book* (1923) Charles E. White, Jr., has a chapter entitled "A Plea for Gardening and Landscaping," which is little more than that—a plea. Henry H. Saylor's *Bungalows* (1911) is only slightly better, giving practical advice on plants that provide color in a garden throughout the year. Indeed, a variety of colors is a must in the landscape architect's mind. There is little evidence that many high-style gardens were ever built, and the ravages of growth and neglect have undoubtedly erased all but a few attempts to put the bungalow in a landscaped setting.

A handkerchief garden next to the front door of a Spanish Colonial Revival bungalow (pages 150–55) is not original but reflects the spirit of the house.

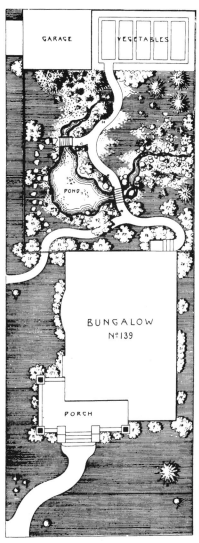

Above: Eugene O. Murmann's *California Gardens* showed a choice of designs appropriate for bungalows, from English to oriental. Each gave bungalow owners ideas for extending their homes to the great outdoors.

Left: Entitled "A Bungalow Home among the Flowers," this period postcard was heavily embellished by an artist to underscore the virtues of California's climate.

THE PORCH

Opposite: Back porches were once used primarily as utility rooms. A view of the woods has replaced mops and brooms on this modern porch in Seattle (pages 100–105), an addition to the owners' log bungalow.

Below: A row of prefabricated bungalows in Roanoke Rapids, North Carolina, all ordered from Aladdin, vividly illustrates an earlier attitude toward front porch sitting. The only thing missing is a swing.

The California bungalow almost invariably had a front porch under a gabled roof. Even eastern and midwestern bungalow designers tried to work a front porch into their plans, although these were eventually enclosed in panels of glass windows when winter gales penetrated the unprotected house. A swing hung on steel chains, and perhaps a couple of wicker chairs rounded out the furnishings. During the bungalow boom the lost art of front porch sitting was still an Edwardian habit.

Just as important as the front porch was one at the rear of the bungalow. It was not used as a place to view the garden but rather as a utility room. In most of the country it was where floor mops and garden and household tools were stored. In California it was also where the washer and hot water heater were located, unless the bungalow had a small basement. Some bungalows boasted a sleeping porch, but most just did not have the room.

THE LIVING ROOM

Bungalow floor plans, drawn for small-sized lots, are extremely economical, sometimes just short of causing claustrophobia. Bungalows that have plenty of space are not really characteristic of the genre. The whole point of the average bungalow was to crowd as much living as possible into a small space.

Most bungalow designers were interested in the architectural features of the living and dining areas. The rest of the rooms—bedrooms, the kitchen, and the bathroom—were clustered around the central space and were treated as simply utilitarian. In this respect bungalow designers were following a tradition established in America as early as the seventeenth century.

Except in the cold Midwest, bungalows usually do not have vestibules or entrance halls. One enters directly into the living room, which is dominated by a fireplace that is often brick but sometimes faced with tile or boulders. In fancier bungalows the fireplace is enclosed in an inglenook with built-in seats on each side. Built-in cupboards with leaded glass doors on each side may frame the fireplace. An arched opening, often with flanking built-in bookcases, leads to the dining room.

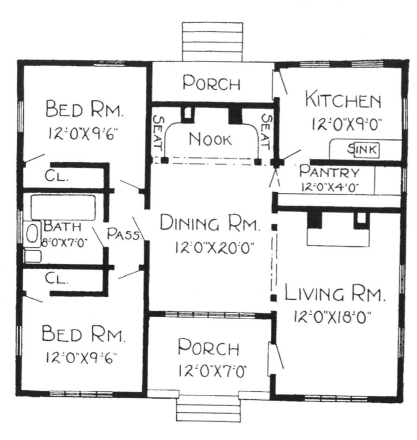

Above: Typical bungalow plans are nothing if not compact and have a fireplace that dominates the living room. Right: This fireplace surround is made of mottled tiles, probably from Grueby Pottery. The rug, while large, is not wall-to-wall.

THE KITCHEN AND DINING ROOM

In the bungalow-building era, the aim was to make kitchens and bathrooms efficient and highly functional. Style was not a major consideration. The kitchen was usually painted white for cleanliness's sake. Contemporary books about bungalows emphasized the need to install all the latest gadgets that would make the woman's workplace more efficient. Cabinetry was built in, although a serviceable kitchen cabinet usually made in Nappanee, Indiana, could also be used. Flooring typically was laid in wood strips, but by the late 1920s colorful linoleum was a popular choice.

Early bungalows had wood-burning stoves, hot-water heaters, and a sink sometimes filled with a hand pump. Later bungalows were much more elaborate. Writing in 1923 Charles E. White, Jr., believed that the ideal kitchen should be fully electrified in the form of an electric range, a portable oven, hot plates, a toaster, a percolator, a chafing dish, and a dish warmer. He even argued for an electric kitchen cabinet that would contain an electrically driven revolving shaft, to which various food preparation devices could be attached. "Your kitchen is your factory," he observed. Refrigerators came late in the period—ice was delivered to some houses well into the 1930s.

Occasionally the dining area was relegated to one end of the living room to give a more spacious feeling, but usually it was a separate room. It almost always included a built-in sideboard and cupboards for dishes and glassware, although in the period revivals of the 1920s the built-ins were often sacrificed for more wall space, and freestanding buffets were used. A chandelier hung low over the dining table. For those who had a concealed, roll-out bed, it was most often installed in the dining room.

Opposite: In tiny bungalow kitchens from the 1920s, every space is put to use. The stove and custom-made hood in a Spanish castle in Altadena, California (pages 168–73), date from the 1930s but are a good compromise with the needs of modern living.

Below: Almost every dining room has a built-in sideboard with leaded glass doors on the overhead cabinets. In this Seattle bungalow (pages 144–47), low wooden wainscoting allows space for a William Morris wallpaper.

BEDROOMS

The bedrooms, usually two, were simple affairs. A random sampling of bungalows suggests that their dimensions generally were roughly eleven by eleven feet—small even allowing for the fact that Americans traditionally have small bedrooms compared to ones found in large houses in Europe.

One characteristic of bungalows was that while the living and dining rooms might be dark, the bedrooms were bright and cheerful. In the period before World War I, when wooden paneling was used in bedrooms, they were generally painted an off-white or cream or similar light color. Some owners today remove layers of paint from their bedroom walls, unaware that they were always painted. And in the 1920s, when paneling was given up for plastered walls, bedrooms were further lightened by the use of bright wallpapers. For Colonial Revival bungalows, figured papers in American colonial patterns were recommended.

Left: The main bedroom of this 1920s California bungalow (pages 168–73), located in a stone tower, is flooded with even more light than most houses of the period. It is also larger and more architectural than standard-issue bungalow bedrooms.

Above: The architect Lawrence Fournier took advantage of a rise on his Minneapolis home site (pages 94–99) to open up this bedroom view. The rectilinear lamp and spindle bed strengthen the bungalow's ties to the Prairie School.

THE BATHROOM

Bungalow builders probably would have preferred to dispense with halls altogether except for one rather important problem: because at the time only one bathroom seemed to be necessary for such modest quarters, and most bungalows had at least two bedrooms, how would residents gain access to the bathroom without a hall? There are, of course, ways such as having the occupant of a front bedroom walk through the living and dining rooms in the middle of the night, but even at the turn of the century this perambulation seemed somewhat primitive. The result was to place the bedrooms and bath close to each other. This could be done only by adding a small hallway. The solution was difficult to carve out of the petite space. One extremely reductionist plan even avoided a hall by eliminating the bathroom. But such extremes were rare, and a small hall was accepted.

The American bathroom had been fully developed in the Victorian era, with only a few finishing touches made in the twentieth century. There was always a tub, wash basin, and toilet. A gift of the 1920s was the tile bathroom—offering color and even mosaics of fish, swans, and water lilies. The bungalow bathroom, like the kitchen, was usually small. And like the kitchen, it has usually been subject to enlargement and remodeling.

Below left: Bungalow bathrooms, like kitchens, were not usually given a great deal of architectural treatment, but they included all the latest appliances—which in this Seattle house (pages 144–47) have an almost sculptural life of their own.

Below right: The hexagonal tile flooring, the tub, and the toilet are original to the house, one of the Lewis Manufacturing Company's mail-order models (pages 148–49). Following the American obsession with cleanliness, everything is ready to be washed down.

THE ATTIC AND BASEMENT

With its low-pitched roof, the California bungalow had little attic space, but other styles called for large attics. The temptation was to add a few dormers and windows in the gables of these houses and create another room or rooms reached by a staircase, usually placed in a corner of the living room.

Following this same logic the builders of the California bungalow often added a small pavilion on the roof of the essentially one-story building to provide a bedroom or billiard room and sometimes even a small bathroom—a practice that gave rise to the name "airplane bungalow."

Except for California-style bungalows, most examples had full basements to accommodate the furnace (generally coal burning), hot-water heater, and laundry spaces. In southern California, where a basement was thought to be unnecessary, water heaters and laundry facilities were usually consigned to the back porch and a floor heater in the living room was often supposed to heat the entire house.

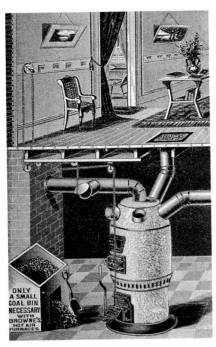

Left: In this ad for household equipment, a frenzied furnace contrasts with the sedate mood upstairs.

Below: A large attic room often provided a space where musicians of the house played without interruption.

FURNISHINGS

It is difficult to generalize about bungalows without immediately making exceptions to the rule. One thing for sure, however, is that wall-to-wall carpet was not recommended. In fact, the pride of most bungalows was their floors, usually of oak, on which oriental or Native American throw rugs were used.

In the period from 1900 to 1915, a great deal of furniture turned out by the Stickley brothers, Charles P. Limbert, the Roycroft Colony, and other manufacturers was used particularly in the West, where it fit in well with Arts and Crafts interiors. Chairs, tables, dressers, beds, servers, desks, and related furnishings were generally in oak. These would be mixed with hand-me-downs, family heirlooms, and anything that the owner of a bungalow might be able to afford.

Rarely were the rooms furnished in any consistent style, although the ideal for the Arts and Crafts interior was carefully described by Charles Keeler, a Berkeley poet, theoretician, and follower of William Morris. In a little book, *The Simple Home* (1904), Keeler describes period furnishings in meticulous detail. Suffice it to say that he suggested "cheerful" paint colors ("buff, brown and red, or occasionally deep blue or rich green"), wall coverings (grass cloth), and curtains ("Chinese denim is very serviceable"), along with oak furniture (in "old Mission" style) and other staples of the Arts and Crafts diet. *The Simple Home* is absolutely *de rigueur* for contemporary collectors who wish to surround themselves with museum-quality furnishings, but today's bungalow owners may find reassurance in the fact that the early-twentieth-century bungalow was eclectic as far as furniture was concerned.

In the 1920s the Stickley (Mission) furniture went out of style even in the California bungalows that continued to be built. In fact, some style manuals urged owners to paint their Stickley furniture white so that it would fit in with the Colonial Revival popular at the time. Furniture styles for bungalows became even more eclectic in the 1920s. It was almost as if Charles Keeler had never written *The Simple Home*.

This living room of Arts and Crafts antiques dealers (pages 126–31) is almost a showcase of period furnishings. To the immediate left is an armchair by L. and J. G. Stickley, while the chairs at right are by J. M. Young Furniture, the Stickleys' competitor in upper New York State. The far lamp has a Bradley and Hubbard base holding a colorful art glass shade. At right is a Prairie lamp.

DECORATIVE ARTS

In *The Simple Home* Charles Keeler advised his readers to purchase paintings by his friend William Keith, but because he suspected that they could not pay Keith's high prices, he suggested that a good effect could be given by using Japanese prints. Although they are "seldom great in idea, and . . . therefore miss the highest quality of art expression," he said, they "are unexcelled for delicacy and subtlety of coloring and grace of form." He also recommended a display of books that "have an ornamental value which is heightened by the idea of culture of which they are the embodiment." Although Keeler's influence did not extend much further than Berkeley, California, his ideas were part of the conventional wisdom that also favored prints of pictures by Maxfield Parrish. Fuzzy photographs of Rheims Cathedral and the Parthenon were also popular. Prints such as these were about all the bungalow owner could afford.

The American passion for high culture was clearly evidenced in the bungalow interior, showing up in copies of Tiffany lamps. Displays of Native American ceramics, baskets, and rugs was also encouraged. But it is impossible to make generalizations about the taste of people who lived in bungalows. Most could not, after all, pay for interior designers to tell them what was correct. They used their own judgment—a policy that all bungalow devotees are well advised to follow.

Opposite: The mantel has always been a good place to display one's taste. Here avid collectors have brought out their vases, all by Van Briggle and in the same shade of green as the tiled hearth (pages 66–67). The painting is in the *plein air* school so popular during the Arts and Crafts era.

Left: William Morris's "Serpent and Peacock" fabric pattern brings a Continental Arts and Crafts flair to a bedroom in a Hollywood bungalow (pages 132–39). The lamp came from a period do-it-yourself kit.

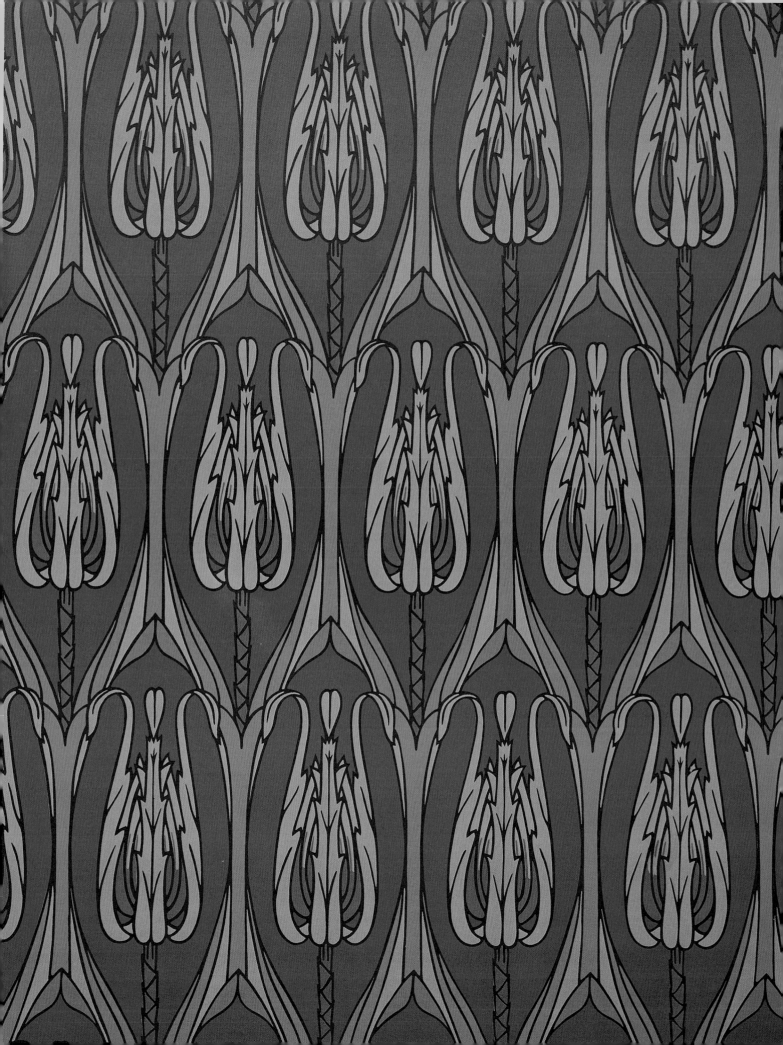

BUNGALOWS REBORN

Bungalow enthusiasts are usually not purists bent on living life as it was in the early part of the century. The people who most revere bungalows have often had to adapt them to their own needs. Kitchens and bathrooms are cases in point, and other rooms often have to be expanded or consolidated to meet the requirements of contemporary living. If such changes were made to a house by Greene and Greene or Frank Lloyd Wright, there might be grounds for protest, but in general a little sensitive remodeling is often required and does not raise serious problems.

The furnishings of the bungalows that follow, arranged by the age of the structures, also reflect the tastes of the present owners and are not necessarily authentic displays of the way things were when the houses were first lived in. There is a strong tendency today, for instance, to use Arts and Crafts furniture although the original owners would have found it too expensive for their purses. The marvel is that old bungalows are such a good background for a variety of tastes.

ALMOST HEAVEN

Bungalow protagonists envisioned whole communities of bungalows, often with a church at the center to serve social as well as religious functions. Befitting such community institutions, they would share with the ideal home many features: a fireplace, movable furniture, good paintings, and rustic surroundings. Set in the residential Pacific Heights section of San Francisco—but not surrounded by bungalows—the Church of the New Jerusalem, built in 1894–95, is such a place.

"The designs of heaven's buildings," wrote Immanuel Swedenborg, the Swedish founder of what is known as the Swedenborgian church, "are so perfect that you would say they represent the very essence of art; and small wonder, since the art of architecture comes from heaven." Swedenborg (1688–1772) saw correspondences between natural objects and spiritual principles. He believed that architecture was the embodiment of the forces of nature and thus evocative of heavenly unities.

This brick church weds Swedenborg's nature theory to the ideas of the Arts and Crafts movement. The great madrone tree trunks that support the roof, their bark left on, suggest Swedenborg's notion of trees corresponding to spiritual knowledge, as do the trees in the lovely garden on the north side of the church. All is Swedenborgian theology.

The design has always been attributed to the San Francisco office of the architect A. Page Brown, but recent scholarship has uncovered information suggesting that the real architect was A. C. Schweinfurth (1864–1900), who was a chief designer in Brown's office. A native of Auburn, New York, and the son of a woodcarver, Schweinfurth was trained in the Boston office of Peabody and Stearns. While there, he was apparently influenced by the even more famous Boston architect H. H. Richardson, whose Romanesque-style round arches Schweinfurth incorporated in the west facade of this church. With its bell tower, the garden elevation seems to have been based on a sketch that Bruce Porter (1865–1953), a leading exponent of the Arts and Crafts movement in the Bay Area, made of an Italian country church in the Po River valley.

Opposite: The massive brick fireplace at the rear of the sanctuary symbolizes the spiritual home. Worshipers would be reminded of this as they entered and left the church.

Below: The chairs, probably designed by A. C. Schweinfurth, have become icons of the Arts and Crafts movement. They appear again at Wyntoon, the house Bernard Maybeck created for the publisher William Randolph Hearst in 1902–3 on the McCloud River in northern California.

Above: Four landscape paintings by the famous California artist William Keith represent the seasons in California and continue the Swedenborgian references inside the church. For the baptismal font, a seashell was used for obvious symbolic purposes.

Right: The sanctuary is a complete statement of American Arts and Crafts and Swedenborgian reverence for wood, signifying natural virtues. Its design followed directly from the church founder's romantic perception of architecture as derived from nature.

Left: The bell tower evokes churches of the Po River valley in Italy as well as California's own Spanish missions. Tile is used both functionally and decoratively.

Opposite: A window of opalescent glass (top left) is one of two designed by Bruce Porter. Located over the pulpit, it shows a dove on the lip of a fountain surrounded by flowers. Porter's other window, on the garden side, depicts St. Christopher holding a young Jesus on his shoulders as they cross a stream. Also in the church is a mysterious chair (top right), for which no one can find any special purpose. The pulpit lamp (bottom left) is eccentric but functional. Still encased in their bark, the evergreen tree limbs of madrone (bottom right) are roughly joined to the walls, supporting a forest-like canopy overhead.

The interior of the church is pure American Arts and Crafts, with wood everywhere. Instead of conventional pews Schweinfurth designed massive chairs; for their detailing he may have sought the advice of the young Bernard Maybeck, who was also in Brown's office at the time. The chairs were crafted by Alexander Forbes, who sent one of them to Joseph P. McHugh in New York in 1894. McHugh used its design as the basis of a line of Mission furniture, thus giving the Arts and Crafts movement its mythical connection to California's Franciscan missionaries.

Joseph Worcester, the church's minister, was important throughout the design process. An amateur architect himself, he undoubtedly recommended domestic touches such as the chairs and the huge brick fireplace—the ultimate symbol of home and family values in a bungalow church. Worcester, a follower of the English Arts and Crafts leaders John Ruskin and William Morris, in 1877 designed as his own home in Piedmont, a single-story cottage that may have been the first bungalow in California.

63

AIRPLANE BUNGALOW

With a cockpit on its roof, which is pitched low with eaves that spread like wings, this house seems to have just landed at an airstrip in front of the glorious San Gabriel Mountains. With porch and roof gables ready for flight, it is a true "airplane bungalow." The property in Altadena, California, was once enormous: A magnificent rose garden was set out on the west and an aviary on the east. To the north was an orange grove. Today all this is gone, subdivided in the American quest to fill up open spaces. Only a diminished but deep front yard remains to suggest the early grandeur.

In front the somewhat cramped quarters call attention to an important fact—the bungalow, especially one of this size, requires a great deal of land. Because it is almost entirely on one floor, it must spread out and is thus expensive to build. Airplane bungalows had to depend on cheap land, something that California had plenty of at the turn of the century when this house was built for the Keyes family in 1911. No one but a wealthy bungalow zealot could have afforded to build such a sprawling bungalow in urban Chicago, for example.

Below: The rhythmic eaves seem to echo the rugged mountains. Although not original, the plantings suit the lines of the house.

Opposite: The east end of the living room is furnished with Stickley and Van Erp pieces, among others. Recently remodeled, this area has modern reproduction lighting.

Overleaf: Dominated by a boulder fireplace with a tile hearth, the living room's west end melds Frank Lloyd Wright influences with Stickley furniture and a Van Erp lamp.

Above: Over the years the kitchen has been completely changed. The gas range dates from later than the house, but it fits in comfortably.

Opposite: The Greene brothers' influence can be seen in other parts of the remodeled kitchen, with its carefully detailed cabinetry. Built-in features were a hallmark of the Arts and Crafts era, allowing furnishings to be part of the architecture, ensuring design unity, and achieving economies of space all at once.

No architect has been found for the house, although it was clearly an architect's work. It certainly was not prefabricated by Aladdin or Sears. Nearby Pasadena has kept permit books since the 1880s, while records in the unincorporated area of Los Angeles County are spottier. But in southern California one almost infallible resource is a journal, *The Southwest Contractor and Builder,* which tried to publish every new building constructed in the Southland. One of the previous owners of the Keyes house attempted to trace it there but failed.

After the Keyes family moved out, the bungalow for a time was occupied by an Australian prizefighter. Then Jackson Gregory, a novelist in the school of Zane Grey, lived in the house and entertained movie luminaries such as William S. Hart, Irving Thalberg, and Will Hays. Over the years the bungalow was badly remodeled, painted, and even changed structurally.

Recent owners have brought it back to life. They have followed the approach that unless a house is a major work of art, the owners may within reason use their own imagination in restoring it. Both occupants have been admirers of the great Pasadena architects Charles (1868–1957) and Henry Mather Greene (1870–1954), so lighting fixtures and other details have been created in the manner of the Greenes. The kitchen is now much more beautiful and functional than the original. Because the owners' personal point of view is moderate and their collections are in keeping with the style, their airplane bungalow remains firmly rooted to its place and time.

THE WRIGHT KIND OF BUNGALOW

Charles E. White, Jr., published a picture of Frank Lloyd Wright's 1907 Tomek house in Riverside, Illinois, in *The Bungalow Book* (1923) and called it a bungalow. But is it really a bungalow? At first glance, it resembles California bungalows, with its strong horizontal lines in the first story, topped by a small, squarish bedroom. Close inspection, however, raises questions: What is the front door doing in the basement? Did Wright (1867–1959) contradict a strong principle of bungalow theorists— that all major functions should be on the first floor? He put the master bedroom, two guest rooms, and a small bathroom in the attic.

The questions can be partially answered by considering the front door in the basement as only a sign of Wright's eccentricity. Besides, it leads to a short flight of steps that rises to the first floor, the important area in any bungalow. Bedrooms were always a nuisance for Wright, who believed that the main purposes of a house were social—centered on the living and dining rooms—and not private, so he tucked the unimportant bedrooms out of sight. Rather perversely, he put in another guest room on the first floor so that the occupant would have to go upstairs to take a bath. This recalls his criticism of Louis Sullivan's great aphorism, "Form follows function." Just as often, Wright observed, function follows form.

Opposite: No matter what size the house, Frank Lloyd Wright liked to put a breakfast nook at the end of the dining room. It was all part of his play with spaces to create architectural sculpture.

Below: Although he posed as a Romantic, Wright loved geometrical order—in this case lining up the living and dining rooms, both of them serviced by an open hall.

Wright nonetheless influenced the bungalow movement, particularly the Chicago phenomenon. The similarities are obvious. Overhanging eaves, hipped roofs, and especially art glass windows are points in common. Even the Tomek house's depressed front door is echoed in many Chicago bungalows, where the basement was often used as an additional apartment for the landlord so that the upper floor could be turned into rental property. The great era of bungalow building in Chicago was during the 1920s, after the Prairie Style practiced by Wright and his contemporaries had run its course, so that it was being adopted as an architecture for the average person. Even the obligatory entrance vestibule in the Chicago bungalow may reflect Wright's distaste for the California habit of entering directly into the living room as much as it does a practical consideration of needing a buffer zone between the harsh midwestern winters and the warm family hearth.

It goes without saying, however, that rarely in southern California or Chicago did designers of bungalows deal with space in the Wrightian manner. Given the close quarters, how could they? A few attempts were made, mainly in the West, to provide cathedral ceilings for living rooms and openings around staircases, but essentially rooms in bungalows were what Wright called boxes.

The Tomek house is small in relation to Wright's best-known works, but in it Wright plays some beautiful games in modeling space. The ceiling that he lowers at two sides of the living room defines the pattern of movement through the house and at the same time leads one's eye to the fireplace—the symbol of family in the Arts and Crafts aesthetic. This effect the architects of the common bungalow would find difficult to manage, even if they could conceive of it.

Above: From this exterior angle, with its first floor topped by a small attic, the stucco Tomek house looks most like a bungalow. The overhanging eaves, punctuated by a squat chimney, provide the sense of shelter for which the Prairie Style is known.

Opposite: Banks of art glass windows line the passage from the dining room to the living room, pouring light into the space. Wright grouped windows to achieve the maximum effect: rather than scattering small windows to punch out a solid wall, he essentially turned the windows themselves into walls of light.

MAXIMUM CABIN

Louis B. Easton (1864–1921), the architect of this 1908 house in Pasadena, California, was a high school manual training instructor in Lemont, Illinois, until health problems brought him west in 1902. His brother-in-law was Elbert G. Hubbard, the founder of the Roycroft Colony in 1893. This noted craft community in East Aurora, New York, pursued Arts and Crafts ideals through handcrafted furnishings and used publications to disseminate the movement's message—one that no doubt was not lost on Hubbard's relative on the other side of the country.

When Easton decided to build a house, he did what many other skilled artisans did when they got into construction that went beyond their experience: he consulted a bungalow pattern book, made some adaptations, and set to work. What appeared was quite conventional, so, according to family lore, he decided to design another house for the property next door, based on his own design theories. It was such a success that for several years he was able to carry on a modest architectural practice in Arts and Crafts houses. He may even have had a hand in the design of Ernest Batchelder's house (pages 80–87) just a few blocks away. Easton advertised himself as a designer who offered a "maximum of effect with the minimum of expense."

The Craig bungalow carries out his motto. From the outside it looks like a modest cabin in the Adirondacks, but the wide front door hints of something special. Simple but well-designed hardware is the first clue. Most bungalows open directly into the living room, but here a hall connects the living room on the south side with the dining room on the north. The living room is doubly notable. It is dominated by an inglenook with built-in seats on each side of the fireplace. But just as striking are the door and window frames and redwood paneling, whose surface was charred and then brushed with sand to bring up the grain. In the dining room the paneling and the built-in sideboard are also of burnt wood.

The present owners—she is a teacher and he is a dealer in Persian rugs—have acquired some Arts and Crafts furniture but in no sense have they tried to make their bungalow a museum. Many rugs and other textiles give elegance to an otherwise calculatedly rustic house.

Unassuming on the outside, the Craig house was intended to fit into the landscape—a characteristic of many Arts and Crafts houses. Through its front door, however, a uniquely detailed domicile awaits.

Above: An enclosed porch looks out into the trees and offers a pleasant work space. Rockers fit well into the bungalow environment.

Left: The wide-swinging front door gives way to a hall, which connects the living room and dining room. The burnt-wood paneling used throughout the bungalow absorbs soft lights and warms the entire space. The Arts and Crafts—style wall sconce is original.

Above: The entrance to the living room affords a view past the hall and into the dining room. Pegs, barely visible in the built-in seat, were trademarks of Louis Easton's work. The owners' rugs and pottery feel like extensions of the walls.

Left: In an otherwise modest room, the inglenook—a favorite Arts and Crafts device—provides real character. A simple but well-designed brick fireplace front is another characteristic Easton touch.

Opposite: The dining room sideboard offers a good demonstration of the rusticity of burnt wood. Frosted glass screens out the house next door.

TRIBUTE TO TILE

A manual training teacher at the Throop Polytechnic Institute in Pasadena, California, Ernest Batchelder by 1905 saw the school's Arts and Crafts curriculum being undermined by the ideas of his friend George Ellery Hale. Hale wanted to turn what was essentially a trade school into a West Coast image of his alma mater, the Massachusetts Institute of Technology. Hale won, and largely under his influence the school became Caltech.

Batchelder decided to purchase property on Pasadena's beautiful Arroyo Seco, where other artists and intellectuals were already congregating. There, in 1909 he built his house and workshop, to which he brought his little coterie of students and set up a school of design. In 1910 Batchelder and his students began designing and producing decorative tiles, a business that in 1920 expanded to a factory near downtown Los Angeles, where it flourished until the Great Depression.

The house as it stands today is two stories and thus not a dictionary-definition bungalow. The building permit, however, reads "6 rm 1 st fr. bung," which seems to have included a partial second-story addition (bedroom and sleeping porch) on the roof. Several years later, after Batchelder had married Alice Coleman, another large bedroom was built upstairs. Nevertheless, the building as originally conceived was intended to be mainly on one floor.

Opposite: From the back yard, french doors lead into the breakfast room and then into the dining room. Mexican tile patterns on the stair riser and hexagonal paver tiles are carried through from the outdoor porch into the house itself. An English table is joined by chairs from the workshop of L. and J. G. Stickley.

Below: Two fountains in Ernest Batchelder's back yard show the tilemaker's art. The earlier one on the left uses facing birds in an interpretation of Byzantine design. The tilemaker's attempt to achieve a Mexican style is shown at right.

Above: The dining room's built-in sideboard holds an
English clock, Tiffany candlesticks, and a Marblehead vase.
The chairs are from the Shop of the Crafters.

Opposite: The living room fireplace was installed in 1912.
Besides Batchelder's own tiles, he inserted a few by Henry
Mercer as a tribute to one source of inspiration.

Above: A heavy redwood door serves as the front entrance. Next to the staircase is a grandfather's clock—which actually belonged to the current owner's grandparents. To the right are two framed pages from an eighteenth-century Qur'an and a modern rug from Granada.

Opposite: Over this window seat Batchelder placed a sconce in his "Birds in Tree" tile design, fabricated by his metalworker, Douglas Donaldson, who lived next door. The frieze above the wainscoting is by the British designer Walter Crane.

The house has an L-shaped plan, one wing of which is the large living room. The other encloses the dining room, kitchen, breakfast room, and study. On the second floor is a sleeping porch and two bedrooms. Like all Arts and Crafts houses, most attention has been given to the living and dining rooms, the rest of the spaces being pleasant but plain. With its cathedral ceiling, the living room is dominated by a large tile fireplace, designed by Batchelder presumably as a wedding present to his wife in 1912. The tiles, in "Viking Ship" and "Italian" (facing birds) patterns, are also his. Near the top are two adaptations in tile of Donatello's "Marzoco" figure, one with a rabbit in its shield and the other with a harp—the former Batchelder's logo and the latter for Alice, a concert pianist and founder of the Coleman Chamber Music Association. A built-in writing desk is at the other end of the room and houses Alice's music cabinet.

Both living and dining rooms are walled with a wainscoting of redwood and Douglas fir up to a plate rail about a foot and a half from the ceiling. The dining room gets it character from a bay window and a rank of french doors. An extremely chaste, built-in sideboard completes the picture. Adjoining the dining room is a breakfast room whose floor and lower walls are covered with Batchelder tiles, both common and decorated.

Above: In a wall at the end of the back yard, a Spanish Colonial Revival fountain was built in the 1920s. Here, under a huge oak, the family could enjoy beautiful summer afternoons.

Right: The brown shingles of the house, which faces the Arroyo Seco, reflect its woodsy setting, while the boulders at the chimney base recall the arroyo from which they came.

STICKLEY'S GARDEN OF EDEN

Craftsman Farms, built in 1910 in Morris Plains, New Jersey, was intended to be a clubhouse for an Arts and Crafts school headed by Gustav Stickley (1858–1942), the furniture maker and founder and editor of *The Craftsman*. His magazine, the leading publication of the Arts and Crafts movement in America, was at first dedicated to the principles of William Morris, the English social reformer who argued for a return to handicrafts to correct the abuses of the industrial age. In the first issue in 1901, Stickley professed a deep belief in Morris's principles, including his socialism, but in the typical American way he quickly tempered his early radicalism with the progressivism of the times. In his factory near Syracuse, New York, Stickley used elaborate machinery that he carefully concealed from photographers. In fact, he became a capitalist, eventually buying a tall office building in New York City.

Craftsman Farms was a temporary haven from the city, within easy commuting distance of New York. Stickley nonetheless erected all the trappings of a rural retreat. When he dropped the idea of an Arts and Crafts community, the house became his home almost by default. Shortly after 1910 he moved his family from Syracuse and himself from an apartment in New York and brought all the Stickley possessions to Craftsman Farms, where they remained until they were sold at auction a few years ago.

In envisioning a school Stickley certainly had in mind Elbert G. Hubbard's Roycroft Colony in East Aurora, New York. He also emulated Hubbard in making an impressive piece of Arts and Crafts architecture the centerpiece. Like most designs published in *The Craftsman*, Stickley gives the impression that he was the designer of his house. He never had any architectural training, however, and because some of the designs were quite complex, it seems obvious that to execute his ideas he used the skills of men and women in his office—who they were we will perhaps never know.

Gustav Stickley's staircase—monogrammed with his "S"—is set against a wall of chestnut logs cut on the property. Both the chairs and the light fixture came from Stickley's United Crafts. His brothers L. and J. G. Stickley designed and produced the tall case clock.

Opposite, top: A large stone fireplace, befitting the rustic cabin, anchors one end of the living room. Its chimney, unfortunately, has been whitewashed, but the copper hood remains unchanged. Almost everything in the room was designed and made by Stickley's firm.

Opposite, bottom: One of the bedrooms is warmed by another fireplace with a copper hood, this one framed in blue tiles that probably came from the Grueby Pottery. The mirror stand is a rare Stickley piece.

Above: The house plans do not show a separate dining room, but when the Stickleys moved in, they turned one end of the living room into a dining area. An array of Arts and Crafts pottery was recently brought in for a special exhibition at the house.

Overleaf: In the spring, when the cherry trees are in bloom, Stickley's Craftsman Farms truly becomes a Garden of Eden.

Although the house is a large bungalow, it hews to the definition, which says nothing about size. The rooms might be somewhat ungainly in proportion, but the furniture and decoration indicate that this was the hub of a Craftsman culture. One of the copper fireplace hoods proclaims an inscription from Chaucer's *Parliament of Fowls:* "The lyf so short, the craft so long to lerne." The other fireplace is inscribed with the phrase, "By hammer and hand do all things stand."

The house is an apotheosis of wood. Logs, which Stickley equated with the simple life, were laid horizontally to make the first-floor walls. Above is a large half story, its long dormer covered with shingles. The chimneys, the kitchen wing, and the substructure of the front porch were built with boulders, and even the diamond-paned windows hint at a purer life before the dawn of the Machine Age.

The interior logs were originally stained a bark color but have been whitewashed in recent times, probably to make the rooms seem brighter. Only the marvelous staircase assembly has escaped the painter's brush. Early photographs show that the original furnishings were almost entirely from the Stickley factory. Books abound.

As if to prove that God was on the side of William Morris, Stickley's financial adventures ended in disaster. He lost his factory and his New York high-rise, and *The Craftsman* folded in 1916, marking the end of the great days of the Arts and Crafts movement. But Stickley lived on in this house until his death in 1942. "This is my Garden of Eden," he said.

BY HAMMER AND HAND

At first sight this Minneapolis residence from 1910 seems to be a typical bungalow, but a closer look divulges the fact that the architect had obviously seen and admired Frank Lloyd Wright's Prairie Style. The window placement has a studied Prairie geometry about it, made more Wrightian by a later owner who inserted art glass in the living room wraparound. Otherwise it resembles many other Arts and Crafts bungalows that were published in Stickley's *The Craftsman*. The stucco siding is common to midwestern houses.

Like typical California bungalows, the front porch opens into a living room that is dominated by a fireplace. On it the present owner has inscribed the phrase, "By hammer and hand do all things stand," which she saw on one of the fireplaces at Stickley's Craftsman Farms (page 88). No one seems to know who painted the mural over the mantel, but it apparently dates from the period during which the first owners lived here. Much of the woodwork seems to have been dyed rather than stained and resembles the crisp, squared-off treatment that Irving J. Gill used in several of his houses in southern California.

Lawrence Fournier (1878–1946), the bungalow's architect and first owner, was a Canadian who moved to Minneapolis in 1908 with his wife, Mary. In 1912 he joined the important office of Purcell, Feick and Elmslie, which was noted for its ornamented midwestern banks recalling the Chicago architect Louis Sullivan as well as for Prairie and Arts and Crafts houses. Later Fournier specialized in banks, but his work never really took off. He designed his house before he worked with William Gray Purcell and George Grant Elmslie, so it has none of the spirit of Sullivan's buildings that Elmslie knew so well.

Fournier's bungalow is in the Utopia addition in north Minneapolis, which was slow to fill up with houses. In spite of easy access to new streetcar lines, it remained relatively unpopulated until the building boom following World War II. For many years the house was part of a bucolic countryside.

Right inside the door is a striking, flowing space—entrance area to living room to dining room—that Fournier must have learned from a firsthand study of Frank Lloyd Wright's work. The identity of the artist who painted the sylvan scene above the fireplace has not been determined, but he or she was certainly acquainted with Arts and Crafts decorative techniques.

by hammer and hand do a

Above: Lawrence Fournier's home could be a typical bungalow except for the wraparound window treatment at the corner. The house retains some of the rural feeling that was more pronounced before the neighborhood was built up after World War II.

Left: In the dining room are a table and chairs reproduced from designs created by Harvey Ellis (1852–1904) for Gustav Stickley. Ellis, an architect, worked for Stickley for less than a year in 1903, but he transformed many of the blocky Mission-style Stickley furnishings and added more delicate lines in keeping with British Arts and Crafts sensibilities.

Above: Built-in cabinets in a bedroom were a compact solution to bungalow living. Following the Arts and Crafts preference for generous amounts of wood in the home, Gustav Stickley's *The Craftsman* promoted woodwork for its "permanence, homelikeness and rich warm color."

Left: Another bedroom is furnished with reproductions of an L. and J. G. Stickley bed and a lamp originally produced by their brother Gustav.

Opposite: The two bedrooms adjoin off the upstairs hall. The upper half story clearly could accommodate sizable sleeping quarters.

MIRROR IMAGE

Opposite: Like a mountain cabin, the old part of this old-new bungalow in Seattle rests in a north woods setting. The large dormers gave the house more vertical space as well as more light for the rooms inside.

Below: The original architect was deeply conscious of the need to harmonize the house with its woodsy surroundings. The rustic porch, with its simple log balustrade and posts, provided a perfect transition between outdoors and indoors and a restful spot to take in the view.

In 1994 this log bungalow in Seattle received the grand prize in the Great American Home Awards presented by the National Trust for Historic Preservation. Restored in 1989 by the firm of Hoshide Williams Architects (Robert Hoshide, principal architect), the 1910 house stands in its own right. But what attracted the unanimous jury was the harmonious addition designed in 1992 by the same firm (Grace Schilitt, project architect). It presents a successful solution to the problem of what to do when you live in an architecturally significant house and you need more space.

With its wood siding, steeply pitched roof, unusually large dormers, and capacious front porch, the bungalow is a classic in the Arts and Crafts style of the Northwest. Although not really suggesting a log cabin, the vertically set logs at the sides of the house establish the theme of rusticity that is carried inside in log beams, from which the bark has been hand peeled. Naturally there is also much wood paneling. A dressed boulder fireplace lights up a rather dark interior.

Above: The fireplace in the old bungalow is not used much today, but the room still functions as an alternative living area. Odd pieces atop the mantel go nicely together.

Left: Like the old fireplace, the new one is constructed of dressed boulders. Built-in shelves flanking the hearth carry out an Arts and Crafts motif. Without resorting to imitation, the new house is completely sympathetic to the old.

Opposite: In the original house, a child's bed fits snugly into the upstairs dormer. Log beams continue the rustic theme while providing key support for the roof. Surely the child who sleeps every night in such dramatic surroundings will develop a taste for the theatrical.

When the owners decided that their growing family required more space, their architect suggested that they make an addition that would be separate from the house but connected to it by an entrance hallway. The result was to enclose a space that now functions as a courtyard. The owners are proud that they selected a sunny space, created many years ago for a Victory Garden, where no ancient trees would have to be cut down for the addition. Here they located a family room bathed in sunlight. At the same time they took details, such as the boulder fireplace in the old house, as models and used them in new ways. The addition shows how to follow the secretary of the interior's guidelines for historic buildings by distinguishing the new from the old while creating a laudable contribution to contemporary architecture.

Above: The painted front door is reminiscent of William Morris's entrance to his Red House (1859) at Bexleyheath outside London. The vertical log wall into which it is set, however, is purely American.

Left: When the original bungalow was built, the architect and client had the delightful sense of humor necessary to design and construct this staircase with log ends, projecting the ultimate in rusticity.

SALUTE TO LUMBER

Fort Bragg, California, is a fascinating company town. Its Union Lumber Company mill, now the Georgia Pacific Corporation, is still the largest employer in the community. When his bungalow was built in 1910–11, Fred C. White was Union Lumber's manager and also president of what is now the California Western Railroad, whose Skunk Train still plies a romantic route through the coastal mountains to Willits in the east.

As is often the case in small towns, few records exist, certainly none that identifies the architect. The careful attention to detail in this house suggests that there was one. Several other houses in town may be by the same architect or builder. The designer, perhaps an understudy of Bernard Maybeck or Julia Morgan, was well schooled in the Arts and Crafts style, choosing floor-to-ceiling redwood paneling throughout the house. The carpenter, Mark Markkula, a Finn, built his own house just across the street from the Whites. He was obviously a master builder in the northern European tradition—the workmanship is elegant.

Unusual for a bungalow, the entrance leads into a front hall that connects the living and dining rooms. Off this is a narrower east-west hall that allows access to the two downstairs bedrooms, a bathroom, a kitchen, and a utilities room. Upstairs are another bedroom and a bath and the inevitable sleeping porch, now glassed in. Added amenities included a maid's room and butler's pantry. This is no average bungalow.

Opposite: A corner of the dining room displays a small built-in server with an overhead cabinet of leaded glass. Although not as elaborate, the carpenter Mark Markkula's detailing is as beautiful as work created by the Greene brothers' carpenters at the Gamble house (1909) in Pasadena.

Below: The Grueby tile surrounding the fireplace is like a tapestry harmonizing with the redwood paneling and beams. The hearth beckons man and beast.

Left: Pocket doors lead to the hall and the dining room. The redwood panel was specially cut so that the grain resembles burled maple.

Opposite: Details were not overlooked in this bungalow. Even a lighting fixture (top left) is surrounded by subtle joinery, and a metal switchplate (top right) is set off against the soft redwood paneling. The cooler in the kitchen (bottom left) creates its own rhythms, as does the electrical fuse box (bottom right). Both are as carefully thought out as everything else in the house.

Left: The house's main facade is oriental as well as Swiss, accented by authentic white window frames. Only a few trees can be found in the area—their absence reflecting a desire for light in a region plagued by overcast skies and fog.

Above: The vine-covered pergola is set above an original redwood deck, where the family could enjoy Fort Bragg's rare sunlight. This garden structure also joins the house to nature, a favored technique of Arts and Crafts proponents.

111

ARROYO REDWOOD

The vast numbers of bungalows built in American cities in the 1910s and 1920s look so common that they seem to have just sprung up right in place. We forget that all of them had designers, even architects, whose names have often been lost in the anonymity of the offices of developers and construction companies for which they worked. It is thus a pleasure when one has a name.

Before coming to San Diego in 1903, Emmor Brooke Weaver (1876–1968) had studied architectural theory and method at the University of Illinois under the supervision of Nathan Ricker. Well educated, his excellent training seems to have been a problem when he joined the prominent San Diego firm of William S. Hebbard and Irving J. Gill. Gill (1870–1936), despite his eminence, was extremely sensitive about his lack of formal architectural education and may have resented Weaver's sophisticated training. Weaver left the firm in 1905 and set up his own practice; later he formed a partnership (1910–12) with John Terrell Vawter, a classmate at the University of Illinois. Together they designed several houses, redwood inside and out, that were simplified Arts and Crafts with overtones of Japanese and Swiss detailing. "There's a sort of mind," Weaver wrote, "that hankers for wooden houses—board and batten—Redwood and Oregon pine. It used to be so, and I guess it always will be."

Allen B. Cook's house, built in 1911 in Mission Hills near San Diego, is one of these. On a narrow lot at the edge of a deep arroyo, Weaver and Vawter designed a U-shaped bungalow that embraced a courtyard. It opens from the dining and living rooms through folding doors, providing essentially another room to be enjoyed in San Diego's mild climate. The bungalow was about 2,000 square feet in area and included four bedrooms, a kitchen, and one bathroom, plus living and dining spaces. The present owner has enlarged the kitchen by incorporating the bathroom space and turning the tiniest bedroom into a bathroom.

All the interior walls are sheathed, floor to ceiling, with wide, vertical redwood planks, making this one of the richest interiors in the American Arts and Crafts movement. Weaver was especially proud of the arrangement of rooms. Of all his houses, he told the present owner, the Cook house was the one that worked the best.

In southern California, residents wanted trees that gave shade and framed an intentionally self-effacing dwelling in the arms of nature. All they had to do was add water and fertilizer to the soil, and almost anything would grow.

113

Above left: The dining room serves double duty as a hallway leading to the two bedrooms at the rear.

Above right: One of the back bedrooms looks into another bedroom across the hall. The house originally had four bedrooms, but the owner has converted one of them into a bathroom.

Left: The living room is small but elegant, mixing Chinese pieces with contemporary furniture. In California Arts and Crafts houses like this one, screens are usually placed inside the window openings.

Opposite: Like other southern California architects, Emmor Brooke Weaver found a patio to be an absolute necessity. For an adjacent bedroom, it brings the outdoors in.

HOME, SWEET BUNGALOW

The Craftsman magazine of September 1911 published an article about a "bungalow worth studying" in Pasadena, California. It was designed, the reviewer said, by Edward E. Sweet and cost only $3,500. A handsome house it was, with foundations of boulders and clinker brick and with low lines and an ample front porch.

The only problem is that while the house appeared about 1911 in *Sweet's Bungalows*, a pamphlet of eighty-five pages of facades and plans, the design was not by Sweet. It most likely was a product of the Pasadena architecture firm of Arthur S. Heineman, for whom his brother Alfred (1882–1974) was chief designer. The bungalow on the cover of the Sweet's book was by Alfred Heineman, by his own admission, and the interiors are characteristic of the Heineman firm (pages 12–13). The Heinemans, who also designed Bowen Court (1912) in Pasadena, often sold their designs to a middleman like Sweet.

Sweet's Plan No. 103 was actually built in South Pasadena and still stands—and it was almost exactly replicated in this stone bungalow in Rochester, New York, probably in 1912, for Arthur Sheffield. The plan was reversed and a back bedroom was omitted, but otherwise it is the South Pasadena house, although the Rochester twin's front porch has been glassed in.

Alfred Heineman loved to create excitement in his living and dining room ceilings. Here he augmented the flat criss-crossed members with slightly arched chestnut beams veneered with gum wood. Commenting on this fact, the writer for *The Craftsman* observed: "The picturesque use of beams throughout the whole house and the harmonious repetition of the curve of them at the windows appeals to one as a unifying note of exceptional charm."

The description of the living room and a "smokery" is amusing for its arch salesmanship and significant clichés: "The arrangement of the interior is no less satisfying, combining comfort, convenience, privacy, simplicity, yet creating a luxurious sense of space. The large living room with its reading table within comfortable proximity to the fireplace, a smaller room joined in social manner, with no sense of lonesome separateness, yet giving certain seclusion to the smokers or perhaps the young students of the household, suggest homeyness, joy of family life." With designs such as this, the California bungalow traveled east.

The present owners use this side porch as their entrance, but the original intention of the architect was that they enter through the large porch across the front, which is now glassed in.

Above: Bungalow residents have always felt comfortable with an eclectic but homey collection of furnishings. In a cold climate like Rochester's, tea by the hearth is a special treat.

Right: At one end of the living room, which has its own fireplace, is a space set off with another fireplace. According to the plans, this is the "smokery." The present owners have furnished it mainly with Stickley reproductions.

Left: Glassed in, the original front porch of the bungalow makes a good place to catch the sun on wintry days in Rochester. Although the furniture is not original to the house, wicker often found a welcome home in Arts and Crafts interiors.

Above: The view from the living room into the side entry shows the beauty of the gum wood that the architects loved to use. Almost identical woodwork can be found in its twin bungalow in South Pasadena, California, built from the same plan.

THE SIMPLE LIFE

Like mail-order houses and Chicago bungalows, this Berkeley bungalow, built about 1912, is simple, plain, and in many ways characteristic of most bungalows in the Bay Area. It will never be listed as a landmark, but it is a good, comfortable home. Sided with stucco, it looks much like many of the other houses on the street. Without having high architectural style, it nevertheless adds to the fabric of its middle-class and socially cohesive neighborhood.

Its owners, modest collectors who are both California preservationists, have furnished the house with period objects. But, like many bungalow owners, they have been affected by the modernist movement of Walter Gropius, Ludwig Mies van der Rohe, and Le Corbusier. A clean and hungry look is given to the interiors of this house by the omission of any window curtains. The furniture and pictures are arranged in an abstract geometrical pattern whatever their age or subject matter. Interior arrangements are far from the haphazard approach that would have characterized furnishings in 1912. An order has been imposed that would never have occurred before the Bauhaus gave rise to the International Style.

Devoted to the bungalow idea, the occupants are nevertheless creatures of their time and express their own taste and point of view. Their house should suggest to other bungalow dwellers that they do not have to be caught in a drive for authenticity. After all, most bungalows are not sacred objects. While their tenants should weigh carefully any exterior changes that would intrude on the neighborhood's cohesion, the interiors are their own and can be manipulated to suit their individual tastes—and whims.

Although simple, this bungalow has notable amenities: a built-in sideboard with overhead cabinets and a built-in writing desk just behind the chair in the foreground. The round dining table softens the house's strong rectilinear lines.

Above: The heavy stone fireplace, with its grandly arched opening, probably came out of a mail-order catalogue that may also have offered fireplaces with cast-stone images of California missions, Prairie schooners, and eucalyptus trees.

Opposite, top: Self-effacing but neat, the bungalow has respectability written all over it and was achieved for little expense. It even has its own redwood tree in the back yard. The battered, or sloping, piers make the entrance the facade's focal point.

Opposite, bottom: From the living room, a hall leads to a small study. The painting, from the California *plein air* genre associated with the Arts and Crafts movement, probably would have been beyond the pocket-books of most bungalow owners.

GRANT WOOD COUNTRY

When built in 1914, this house in Ottumwa, Iowa, was brown-shingled on the exterior with a white stucco base and trim. It was set on an acre of land with beautiful terraces extending down to a garden. At some time, probably in the 1920s, when many people wanted their homes to look "colonial," it was painted white.

The house was designed by Henry Throne, about whom little is known. His clients were Louise and Lester Hardsocg, whose family had been successful at running a small-scale industry in southern Iowa during the late nineteenth century. Considerably larger than the conventional bungalow, it was expensively finished with quartersawn oak woodwork and floors and built-in features such as a sideboard and bookcases. A special touch is elegant art glass doors throughout the house, possibly crafted in Chicago.

The Hardsocgs lived in the house for sixty-five years, until 1979, and kept it up in a fine manner. The two families that followed them made only cosmetic changes, such as glassing in the side porch and putting down wall-to-wall carpet. The present owners are antiques dealers and have furnished it with pieces by the various Stickleys, Charles P. Limbert, and their contemporaries.

The house has five bedrooms. One of them in the half story upstairs is still decorated in its original colors of white, mustard, and a pin-stripe of dark apricot. The living room is surprisingly light and airy, an effect gained by eliminating curtains. As with all good bungalows it is dominated by a fireplace, in this case made of richly colored tapestry brick. Once in the country but now inside the boundaries of Ottumwa, it still gives the impression of a farmhouse in a Grant Wood painting.

Chicago's infatuation with bow windows made its way to Iowa. Here, the windows are wider than those in the usual Chicago bungalow, even though this house is far from the street. Ash trees help relate the building to nature.

Above: The dining room is screened from the living room with art glass doors. Glass on the sideboard carries a stylized design of two Indian feathers. Although Frank Lloyd Wright designed art glass at the time, it is doubtful that Ottumwa architects did.

Opposite, top: Tucked in under the eaves of the roof, the upstairs bedroom is now being used as a study. Some of the original painted decoration shows in the angled ceiling. The owners have matched its colors in the throw rug.

Opposite, bottom: For a bungalow this living room is large. Its fine examples of American furniture include a chair by L. and J. G. Stickley. The fireplace is faced with an unusual tapestry brick, whose varied shades of red and gray give warmth to the room.

Above: A simple paneled door opens into a compact bedroom, lighted by a lamp with a lacy art glass shade.

Right: The side porch was originally open, but because midwesterners tend to want more interior space, it was enclosed. From the rockers and wicker furniture to the sconce and Native American rug, the furnishings project an Arts and Crafts sensibility.

MOVIELAND MAGIC

Hollywood, California, is notable for street after street of bungalows and bungalow courts. The town's growth in the 1910s and 1920s, thanks to the expansion of the movie industry, guaranteed that many homes for movie "extras" and other employees of the motion picture studios would have to be built. The southern California style of living closely identified with the California bungalow can still be found there.

This 1915 bungalow is typical of many in Hollywood neighborhoods—a more than adequate front porch set across the first floor and a rather large half story cutting across the building. It is the domain of an avid collector of Arts and Crafts and objects from related movements such as the Vienna Secession. The owner, Ronald Bernstein, is obviously interested in bringing together specimens of the period from 1900 to 1920 that are rarely experienced in the usual Arts and Crafts interior.

Left: Even if the space is cramped, every bungalow must have its garden. This one even manages a tiny pool with water lilies and a galaxy of subtropical plants. Although the house is not near the mountains, the boulders give the necessary rugged look.

Above: Just a simple stucco house with the usual adequate front porch, the bungalow's facade hardly prepares visitors for the treasures that lie inside. The landscaping is obviously contrived to contrast with the house's understated architecture.

Above: The dining room is almost gardenlike, bathed in warm light from windows and a door. High wainscoting provides a resting place for selected decorative objects.

Opposite: The portières between the living and dining rooms can easily be closed to create more intimate spaces. In colder climates, they helped protect against drafts.

Preceding pages: Everywhere one looks in the living room are distinguished examples of Arts and Crafts furnishings. The wooden door and window surrounds are echoed in the carefully collected furniture.

The front door opens directly into the living room, which centers on a fireplace with a tile surround. To the right is a settle manufactured by Gustav Stickley's United Crafts, and on the table is an elephant-foot lamp, another Stickley piece. The mantel holds two Minton vases in Vienna Secession designs. On the center table is a large Grueby vase placed on an embroidery by the Royal Society, over which a Dufner and Kimberly chandelier is hung. The L. and J. G. Stickley desk against the wall facing the front door is flanked by two straight chairs designed by the English Arts and Crafts leader M. H. Baillie Scott. The rug was designed in the "Donnemara" pattern by C.F.A. Voysey, another prominent English Arts and Crafts designer.

Adjacent to the door leading into the dining room is an unusual chair by the Arts and Crafts furniture designer Charles Rohlfs of Buffalo, New York, next to which is a Rookwood garden urn. The portières are Secession style, as is the cloth on the Stickley dining table. The rug is a rare Stickley "zigzag" pattern. The chandelier is by Handel. The owner has taken a straightforward bungalow and furnished it with objects that are unusual for a bungalow—even in Hollywood. Every piece is museum quality.

Opposite: The owner's collection has found a good home throughout the bungalow. A Minton vase (top left) is in the style of the Vienna Secession movement, while an elephant-foot lamp (top right) was produced in Gustav Stickley's workshop. The built-in sideboard (bottom left) holds rare Arts and Crafts items. In the vintage bathroom (bottom right) are a pedestal basin and a clawfoot tub.

Above: A wood stove would never do in a functioning bungalow kitchen, so the owner found a late-1920s gas range and a refrigerator to match. This is a compromise with history that many bungalow owners have made. Modern appliances also look good in many bungalows.

ROSE VALLEY RUSTIC

With financial assistance from Edward Bok, founder of the *Ladies' Home Journal,* the Philadelphia architect Will Price and others in 1901 established a utopian Arts and Crafts community outside Philadelphia. At Rose Valley, as it was called, craftsmen were to labor "filled with a yearning and a pity for those whose work and environment were not so happy," Price suggested. They did this for about five years until, unhappy with their own working conditions, they closed most of the furniture and other crafts workshops. Community residents remained, pursuing Arts and Crafts ideals through activities such as theater and musical performances.

In 1917 the noted architect William Gray Purcell (1880–1965) built his summer bungalow in the old Rose Valley colony. Purcell was one of the leading Prairie School architects in the Midwest. Associated in Minneapolis with George Grant Elmslie (1871–1952), one of Louis Sullivan's most important collaborators, Purcell's practice was mainly in domestic architecture, but the firm also designed banks, churches, and even courthouses throughout America's heartland. The partnership with Elmslie broke up in 1922, but as early as 1917 Purcell had moved to Philadelphia to become advertising manager for Alexander Brothers, a firm that went bankrupt in 1919.

In plan, Purcell's Rose Valley bungalow was a simple inverted T-shape, essentially one room across the front. "Bed closets" occupied two corners of the living room. The essential fireplace came with an overmantel of wood inlaid in a geometric pattern interrupted amusingly by a tree branch and a squirrel. Doors on each side of the fireplace led to the kitchen and bathroom. Off the living room was a wing enclosing a sleeping porch and a roomy storeroom.

In the 1950s major changes were made to the house to convert the kitchen into a bedroom and to enclose the sleeping porch to make a dining room. The storeroom was turned into a small kitchen, and a large living room was added. Purcell's style was maintained in the additions, including his ornamental rafter ends.

The present owners are major collectors of Walt Disney memorabilia. Because their archives are beginning to fill the house, they are in the process of creating another addition. Without slavishly imitating Purcell's style, they are ensuring that the new work is sympathetic to it.

Above: In the 1950s the original sleeping porch overlooking the garden was walled in to create a dining room. The flamingoes are an even newer addition.

Opposite: The slender stem of the T-shaped house, essentially a one-room bungalow, started out as a wing containing a storeroom at the end (now the kitchen) and a sleeping porch. In the adjacent main part of the house, located in the cross of the T shape, were the living room, kitchen, and bathroom.

Above: Some of the Walt Disney memorabilia that the owners have amassed over the years can be seen in the bungalow's 1950s addition. Art glass panels on the door were relocated from the original house.

Right: The added wing now houses a den. The owners' furnishings include reproductions of numerous period pieces, from an Arts and Crafts sofa seen here to Frank Lloyd Wright's famous origami-like "butterfly" chairs found at Taliesin West.

Opposite: A reproduction of a Charles Rennie Mackintosh dining set occupies center stage in the dining room, formerly the sleeping porch. Its tall-back chairs draw the eye upward toward the pitched ceiling. The original storeroom in the rear became a kitchen in the 1950s.

BORN AGAIN

When Olivia Dresher bought her bungalow in 1992, it was close to ruin. "It was a complete disaster," she told a reporter for the *Seattle Times* in 1994. "Wires were hanging everywhere, ceilings were falling down, woodwork was painted over. We truly rescued a dead house." Dresher essentially rebuilt this house in Seattle's Wallingford neighborhood, taking ideas from what remained and projecting what the house might have looked like when it was built in 1918.

After conducting historical research into the house, she was not afraid to interpret the facts as she found them. In the kitchen, for example, the only shard of the past was a short rank of cupboards whose design she used as a model for new carpentry. She drew the line at contemporary design in the kitchen. "All the latches, even the switch plates, are old-fashioned. I don't have anything modern in the kitchen—no garbage disposal or dishwasher. I love washing dishes by hand. And I have a 1923 stove."

The contractors, Calvin Chambers and Dennis Monicatti, estimated that the basic reconstruction would take six months. But they discovered that their client was not just a fixer-upper but a person who wanted everything to be done exactly right so that she would never want to move. As a result, the house was finished only after twenty months, at almost four times the original estimate.

With the help of her interior designer, Laurie Taylor of Seattle, Dresher searched the country for antiques and reproductions that would suit the house. Embroidered portières, a Mackintosh rose stencil, a new front door, handblocked wallpaper, and a wide range of hardware were purchased from suppliers coast to coast. Now the house looks better than it did when it was first built. For her painstaking efforts Dresher received first prize for interior rehabilitation in the 1994 Great American Home Awards administered by the National Trust for Historic Preservation.

Like the entire house, the fireplace survived years of neglect but needed only some repointing of the bricks to return it to useful service. The remainder of the living room was reconstructed so well that one cannot tell what is new and what is old. A bit of new ivy stenciling can be seen in the wall frieze beyond the bookcase. The rocker is an old L. and J. G. Stickley piece.

Above: The kitchen came close to being reconstructed from scratch, but the result looks almost right for 1918. The curtains are a Morris design.

Right: The clawfoot tub was purchased to replace one that was too damaged to use. The bathroom's wood paneling also is new.

Opposite: By 1918 Craftsman browns were being replaced by lighter shades of paint such as the owner used in renovating her house. Except in the East, the front porch was an essential feature of bungalows.

A HOUSE BY MAIL

In a city known more for its white marble monuments, Washington, D.C., and its suburbs have a surprising number of mail-order houses. Sears bungalows and grander houses line streets in nearby areas such as Arlington, Virginia, and Takoma Park, Maryland. Bungalows abound in the city itself, including the northwestern neighborhood of Chevy Chase. There, about 1919, this bungalow arrived ready to assemble from Lewis Manufacturing of Bay City, Michigan. The choice must not have been difficult for the owners: the model is named the Chevy Chase.

"There are some home sites into which a long, low-lying house just seems to fit, and for them no design could be better than our Chevy Chase," concluded the Lewis catalogue in 1922, three years after the house was first offered. The price then was $3,537, according to a copy in the collection of the Bay County Historical Society, which has documented the Lewis story in its book *Historic Architecture of Bay City, Michigan*. A spinoff of the Aladdin Company in 1913, Lewis lasted until 1973 and shipped a total of 60,000 "ready-cut" houses. The Chevy Chase was not among its most popular models and was discontinued after 1924.

The generous plan called for five bedrooms, two downstairs and three upstairs. The two on the first floor have been converted into a study and den, which can be closed off from the living room with a pocket door. Beyond, the former sleeping porch today serves as a cozy design studio filled with sunlight and a view out into the bucolic city lot.

Opposite, top: The builder reversed the plan of the house from the view in the mail-order catalogue, placing the living room on the side of the house shown. It opens to the dining room and then the kitchen, while the main bedroom is tucked into the front dormer upstairs. The stonework was left to the builder, who produced an assertive entrance for this property, located on a corner and up a small rise.

Opposite, bottom: Lewis touted the house's "unusually large" porch space—a front veranda, a sleeping porch downstairs, and a third porch off the kitchen—and suggested that it would appeal to people who like the outdoors. One of its current owners, a landscape designer, certainly does and has taken special care with the garden.

Left: The spacious living room "betokens comfort and hospitality," according to the catalogue. Seven windows light the space, including two "old-fashioned casements" flanking the stone fireplace.

HISPANIC HACIENDA

Architecture and land speculation have gone hand in hand, particularly in California, where art and money were always close friends. A development venture probably produced this Spanish Colonial Revival bungalow in San Diego, designed by William Templeton Johnson (1877–1957) in 1921. The house was registered in the name of his wife, Clara, because of its speculative nature. Neither one ever lived here.

While at Columbia University in 1906–7, Johnson was told by one of his professors that if he really wanted an architectural education, he must go to the Ecole des Beaux-Arts in Paris, like other young Americans from Richard Morris Hunt and H. H. Richardson to Bernard Maybeck, Julia Morgan, and Louis Sullivan. Clara was a wealthy heiress, so William was able to go with all expenses paid by his wife.

After two years at the Ecole he returned to the United States to practice in New York. Clara, however, decided to vacation in the West and, after seeing San Diego, bought property on Coronado Island and determined that "the West was best." The couple moved to San Diego in 1912, and William became a licensed architect the next year.

At first he worked in the Arts and Crafts mode and designed buildings such as the Francis Parker School (1913–15). But for the Panama-California International Exposition, held in San Diego in 1915, he designed the Fine Arts Gallery (now the city art museum) at the bidding of Bertram Grosvenor Goodhue (1869–1924), the fair's principal planner. The experience converted Johnson to the Hispanic mode. From then on he was happiest when he was working in stucco and tile.

Johnson's stucco bungalow is a modest but fine example of his later style. He seems consciously to have avoided any taint of the modernist movement except in the bathroom and kitchen. It was the Spanish Colonial Revival that moved him. The present owners, themselves admirers of the taste of the 1920s, have furnished the house and fine gardens in line with his intentions.

Filled with sunshine, the living room dramatizes the change of taste from the woodsy Craftsman architecture of the early twentieth century to the Colonial Revival of the 1920s. Bright-colored fabrics suddenly came into fashion, and a more carefree approach took over. Although the house's exterior is Spanish, the interior—except for the beamed ceiling—could be an East Coast colonial.

151

Above: The front hall leading to the living room is narrow and indicates a change in the earlier attitude toward halls—essentially that they should be avoided. This one has an appropriately Spanish arched ceiling and appropriately eclectic furnishings.

Right: The present owners have obviously kept their eyes open for furniture made by Grand Rapids companies in the 1920s and, while using modern devices such as the wall lamp, understand the 1920s taste for mixing items in an orderly way.

Above: In Spanish Colonial Revival houses the front porch disappeared and was replaced by a patio. This space may not have been used much for sitting because a second, more private patio lies at the rear.

Left: Using red tiles, an arched doorway, and proper Hispanic features, the architect knew how to evoke the right picturesque mood.

Opposite: Set into a window hood, a detail catches the Islamic interest in splashing a colorful emblem on a neutral surface. The bungalow reflects southern California's identification of itself as the New Iberia, but the relation to Islam is remote.

CHICAGO BUNGALOW BELT

In "Chicago and the Bungalow Boom of the 1920s" *(Chicago History,* Summer 1981), Daniel J. Prosser observes, "For those who grew up between Halsted and Ashland on the Far South Side or in the outlying sections of Jefferson Park, the bungalow is as familiar as an old green and white CTA car. Even suburbanites who travel through the Northwest Side on the Milwaukee Road can hardly fail to notice the small, hip-roofed brick houses which line block after block of the area. For good reason, more than one observer has referred to the 'bungalow belt' bounding long stretches of the city limits." Citing Homer Hoyt's *One Hundred Years of Land Values in Chicago* (1933), Prosser notes that in 1925 at the height of the boom, 9,371 single-family dwellings, most of them bungalows, were built in Chicago alone, with the number tapering off in 1929 to 2,931. About 100,000 bungalows were built in Cook County during the decade.

That this enormous growth occurred in the prosperous 1920s is significant, because it determined the design of the Chicago bungalow. Land values had gone up, so the conventional city lot was pared down to thirty or thirty-five feet wide. To put a bungalow on a narrow lot, therefore, the house had to be long and narrow. Back and front yards were cramped by California standards. The new popularity of the automobile required a garage and either a driveway at the side of the house or an alley in the rear, further limiting the Chicago bungalow's dimensions.

It is not so easy to explain why these bungalows were usually sided with brick rather than wood and usually constructed of masonry. After all, Chicago was the birthplace of the balloon frame and had a long history of wood-sided houses. But the building codes encouraged brick. The Prairie Style example promoted by Frank Lloyd Wright and other midwestern architects may have had something to do with the choice of materials, because Wright and the other Prairie architects liked brick and stucco. Of course, keeping in mind the bungalow's mission, brick did reflect permanence and stability in a rapidly changing society—although in southern California, where the same social goals existed in an area of few forests and a great many termites, brick was almost never used.

The Prairie Style architect's fondness for art glass is also reflected in the humblest of Chicago bungalows. With the possible exception of Vancouver, British Columbia, nowhere else can so much art glass be found in bungalow windows. Unfortunately a great deal of this glass is being ripped out and sold to dealers and collectors to pay for new roofs and other repairs—a phenomenon not limited to the common bungalow but affecting other historic houses as well.

Chicago's simple bungalows were a great place to come home to. The facade of this one—memorable because there are so many like it in the Midwest—is the embodiment of the Chicago style, just as indigenous to its place as the California style is in the West. The sunroom acknowledges a desire to commune with nature while being protected from its worst attributes.

Typical plans for Chicago bungalows are close to those used for California bungalows. Entry, however, is often through a vestibule rather than straight into the living room. The dining room is a little smaller than the living room and is separated from it by an arch. Behind it is the kitchen. Almost always the bedroom and bath are reached through a door at the back of the dining room or at the front of the kitchen. Chicago bungalows usually have full basements and attics with dormers toward the street.

As Daniel Prosser notes, in spite of their apparent inexpensiveness, these bungalows represented a heavy investment for their owners, who were often weighed down with mortgage payments that would have been hard to meet even with full employment. Then came the Great Depression. These were the homes that so many people of limited means lost in those troubled times.

PRAIRIE LIGHTS

Old timers in this Chicago neighborhood say that this 1927 bungalow was built on speculation. Several others similar in style and plan were built nearby, although this may be one of the best of the lot. As is often the case, the name of the architect is unknown.

Like so many Chicago bungalows, its walls are yellow brick. The roof, now covered with composition shingles, was once tiled. The dormer that usually suggests an upstairs really lights only the attic. The house's chief glory is its bow window, which allows sunlight to pour into the living room. It also permitted the designer to use art glass that was enchantingly conceived to echo details in the rest of the house, arches in particular.

Although the art glass and the broad reach of the eaves are reminders that the Prairie Style was popular well into the 1920s, the fireplace and its flanking built-in cupboards are clearly inspired by period architectural revivals of the time, in this case the Colonial Revival. While painted white to resemble the Georgian style, they are as beautifully crafted as anything in the pre–World War I period. The Arts and Crafts movement did not close up shop in 1917.

The present owners have consciously added their own eclecticism to this congeries of taste by furnishing the house with mainly Victorian pieces, the point being to show from what milieu the bungalow came. "I love this house," says the male of the household. There are many comparable bungalows in Chicago neighborhoods that need the same loving attention as these owners have given—care that comes from the tenant and is not created by an outsider brought in to decorate the place.

Opposite: In this corner of the dining room, the architect clearly had the Colonial Revival in mind and mixed it nicely with Chicago art glass. The little garden in the south window is an echo of the traditional relationship of the bungalow to its natural surroundings, although in this case the garden must be brought inside.

Left: With its street-facing dormer, a Chicago tradition, this bungalow represents the city's finest. The bow window in front gives the residents a chance to survey the passing scene.

Above: Looking from the dining room
into the living room, the owners'
Victorian furniture is set against
Georgian arches and Prairie windows.
Bungalows made good homes for
eclectic combinations like these.

Left: The bow window collects the
sun and brings it inside, where
it is welcome on a cold Chicago day.
Colonial-style Palladian arches used
throughout the house are repeated
in these fanlights, but the art glass
below is pure Prairie School.

Above: An arch leading to the small
entrance hall frames the high win
dow, whose art glass arch is exactly
proportioned to the door opening.

Right: The contrast between the
Victorian furniture and the elegant
colonial cupboards and mantel
is dramatic and intended. This is
a glorious example of American
eclecticism, right down to the
antimacassars.

HANSEL AND GRETEL

Still picturesque, this house in Riverside, Illinois, was even more so when built, its undulating roof covered with shingles in swirling patterns to imitate English thatch. It was probably intended to be a Cotswold cottage—style bungalow but turned so cute that it became Hansel and Gretel instead.

Roscoe Harold Zook, who was undoubtedly the architect of this house, was graduated from Chicago's Armour Institute (now Illinois Institute of Technology) in 1889. He lived most of his life in Hinsdale, Illinois, and is presumed to have designed this confection about 1925. He was responsible for more than thirty period revival houses there, several of them resembling this bungalow. One of his admirers exclaimed, "What Frank Lloyd Wright was to Oak Park, Zook was to Hinsdale!" He worked in the office of Howard Van Doren Shaw, one of Chicago's most respected architects. When he established his own office, Zook was enormously successful in finding clients who recognized his talent. He fit beautifully into the 1920s desire to have well-crafted houses in the spirit of the earlier Arts and Crafts movement but provided more pizzazz than the houses shown on the pages of Gustav Stickley's *The Craftsman*.

Zook created rather florid designs in Hinsdale as well as in other Chicago suburbs, including Riverside. He often devised a rather strange interpretation of the Cotswold style, of which this is a fine example. Accounts describing his work almost always say that he loved to make a V-shaped window that projected at the front like a ship's prow. One is notable here. Zook liked to bring the eaves of his roofs close to the ground. Notice the front elevation. Above all, he insisted on fine craftsmanship and careful detailing, both conspicuous here.

For such a small house the interiors are unusually sophisticated. A cathedral ceiling framed in cypress gives the living room a feeling of spaciousness. Original chandeliers in the living and dining rooms are 1920s period pieces and would be just as appropriate in a Spanish Colonial Revival bungalow in southern California or a Tudor house on Long Island. As the depressed Tudor arches show, for all its concern with styles the taste of the 1920s was hardly pure. The present owners have followed suit, mixing 1920s floor lamps with contemporary art.

What they are still looking for is a mark that would establish this as a Zook design. Whenever he thought that he had done a good job, he would sign the building somewhere with a spider web. Sometimes he fashioned a fire screen with a web on it. Once or twice he designed a front window with a spider pattern in leaded glass. As yet the owners have been unable to find the evidence that would clinch their claim.

Above: Typical of fixtures designed for a variety of architectural styles in the 1920s, these period chandeliers are faintly medieval-looking.

Opposite: At the entrance, the roof swoops down low to offer welcome shelter. The multipaned front window juts out like the prow of a ship. Both of these features are known signatures of Roscoe Zook, the probable architect of the house.

Above: Seen from the dining room, the entrance vestibule is framed in a depressed Tudor arch. This suggestion of a hallway quickly disappears in the traditional bungalow effort to achieve more living space.

Right: Entering the house, the living room is to the right and the dining room straight ahead. The floor lamps, tables, and straight chairs are good examples of 1920s taste. Everything in the bungalow is held together by the Tudor arches.

CASTLE IN SPAIN

Poised on the edge of a canyon in Altadena, California, with its tile roof and round-arched windows, this house seems to be Spanish Colonial Revival in style, but the dressed-boulder exterior gives it a "castle in Spain" look, on a bungalow-sized scale. To no one's surprise, its builder and first owner, M. W. Wilkins, was a stonemason. Sometime around 1925 he began by constructing a stone garage in which he and his wife lived while he built their house.

The architect, whoever he or she was, had absorbed the 1920s image of Spain. On the exterior, iron rods above the den window show where canvas drapes once hung. Old photographs document that the living room window was shaded by an awning supported by spears, the perfect Hispanic touch.

The somewhat fortresslike exterior masks the fact that the interior is flooded with cheerful light during the day. On entering the house one comes almost immediately to a tiny den made to look even smaller by a massive boulder fireplace beautifully crafted by Wilkins. The den was his sanctum sanctorum. Apparently he had a bearskin rug on the floor and a spittoon conveniently placed near his easy chair, a scene that the present owner has decided not to replicate.

The living room is larger, a high ceiling giving it a more expansive look. The handsome dressed stone fireplace may have been cut from one huge boulder. An arch leads into the small dining room. A little study was annexed to it by a latter-day occupant who closed in a side porch, incorporating it into the interior to give a greater feeling of space.

The kitchen is minuscule but well designed. Behind it is another room that was Mary Wilkins's chiropractic clinic. Perhaps the loveliest room in the house is its single bedroom (pages 48–49), given character by a tower window almost like a Queen Anne house. The view from it across the garden is spectacular.

Wilkins also probably built the gardens in both the front and back yards. It is usually difficult to recreate an old or historic landscape because over the years it is uprooted, dies, or becomes a wilderness, but here it was easy to reconstruct the idea if not the species of plants. Walks, seats, ponds, and bridges were built in concrete fashioned to look like branches of trees with the bark left on, a form of rustication that was borrowed from the eighteenth-century vogue of the picturesque.

Above: Painted a clear 1920s blue, the arched front door is typically Spanish Colonial Revival in style. Its center grille suggests that, in spite of the entry's forbidding stone frame, there is light inside.

Opposite: Few bungalows are sited so beautifully. The fortresslike exterior echoes the rugged backdrop. With its logs of concrete devised to resemble tree branches, the garden adds to the house's sublime mood.

Left: The arched doorway between the living and dining rooms frames the impressive stone fireplace, supposedly built from fragments of one huge boulder. Afternoon sun adds to the room's warmth and separates it from the softly lighted dining room.

Above: Once a porch, the stone-walled study was glassed in by a later owner to give the adjoining dining room a more spacious feeling. Because it was once outside, it brings the exterior inside and creates a little cave—with a view.

Overleaf: The rear of the bungalow looks out over a garden, with more concrete ornaments, and into a large canyon and the mountains beyond. In the stone tower is a large bedroom whose windows flood the room with morning sunlight.

MAYBECK WITH A VIEW

Bernard Maybeck (1862–1957), the architect of this spectacularly sited bungalow in Berkeley, is one of the few California architects who have been recognized by the eastern scholarly establishment. His fame rests primarily on two buildings—the First Church of Christ, Scientist (1910), in Berkeley and the Palace of Fine Arts (1913–15) for the Panama-Pacific International Exposition held in San Francisco in 1915.

Maybeck was the son of a New York cabinetmaker who was sufficiently well off to finance his education at the Ecole des Beaux-Arts in Paris. At that time the Ecole sheltered the finest—in fact, the only—architectural school in the world to teach the importance of reason, function, and order in architecture. Maybeck was a Romantic at heart and seems to have bridled under these restrictions, but he never really broke with the Beaux-Arts method. He once told a newspaper reporter that he and Frank Lloyd Wright were both Greeks, a great insight into his own work as well as Wright's.

Left: The entrance court is typical Berkeley—understated architecture and sensational greenery. It is a wonderful prelude to a dramatic interior.

Opposite: Inside, the bungalow explodes with a sense of spaciousness, aided by cathedral-like vaulted ceilings. Maybeck took the living room window design from factory architecture, a detail he used also in his Christian Science church in Berkeley. The cat has decided that there is no sense competing with the house's view of the Golden Gate.

Above left: At this corner of the living room near the kitchen, the present owners put a table. Because Maybeck did not design a breakfast room for the house, it is here that they have their *petit déjeuner* overlooking the Golden Gate.

Above right: A rather mad staircase leads to the loft that is now the master bedroom. Under it is the door to the dining room.

Opposite: The rosettes at the top of the fireplace probably once decorated the organ pipe screen of Maybeck's Christian Science church in Berkeley. He designed the andirons for another house.

Overleaf: On one door of Maybeck's somber, medieval-style dining room, once the main bedroom, a copper plate has been hung—it covers a hole made when a previous owner installed a loud speaker.

Florence and John Tufts (he was a dentist) were both well-known artists and extremely active in the cultural life of Berkeley. They were important clients, having chosen Maybeck to be their architect twice before. The bungalow he designed for them in 1931 is somewhat of a Cotswold cottage. Outside, stucco and brick cover Maybeck's peculiar interpretation of balloon-frame construction, which is exposed on the interior walls. The story is that he stood in the living room as the house was being framed and said, "Now wouldn't it look nice if we filled in the spaces between the boards with plaster?" And so it was done.

A small garden and a lateral porch open into a short hall. The kitchen is on the left, and the maid's (now guest's) room is on the right. Then comes the great visual explosion of the living room, its large window framing a view of the Golden Gate. The vaulted ceiling is made of cedar boards stained to look like poured concrete. As if he were a little concerned that his framing was too fragile, Maybeck pulled together the building with tiny tie-beams, again asserting an interest in exposed construction and making it part of the visual experience.

Maybeck was always fond of generous fireplaces. Here he gave the great chimneypiece a special air—setting on the lip a metal plate salvaged from the French pavilion at the 1915 exposition. Five unevenly spaced tin rosettes decorate the space where the chimney meets the ceiling. At the north end of the living room is a door leading into what was once the master bedroom and is now the dining room. A staircase modeled in Maybeck's mannerist way leads to what was originally the studio but that serves the present owners as a master bedroom. Overall, little in this wonderful house, including the kitchen, has been changed.

Left: The living room is not huge, but Bernard Maybeck made its space speak loudly. The high ceiling, the tall windows, and the unusual fireplace contribute to this effect.

Opposite: In the kitchen (top left), the counter is almost exactly as Maybeck designed it, and the oven (top right) is original. A distinctive door handle (bottom left) occurs throughout the house. It seems Japanese but is a Maybeck creation. A fountain (bottom right) is a later addition to the garden designed by the architect.

COTTAGE FOR A SQUIRE

Biddestone, the 1937 house built in Farmington Hills, Michigan, for Edward Moseman, a successful lawyer from Pontiac, is outside the period usually associated with the bungalow. It shows that the bungalow lived on, in this case as a Cotswold cottage. Moseman commissioned Marcus Burrowes (active 1890–1947), a prominent southeastern Michigan architect for millionaires, to fashion a house that would commemorate his family's English heritage. Biddestone was the English village from which the Moseman family came.

Burrowes gave Moseman everything he asked for. Seeing a wonderful Richardsonian Romanesque federal building being demolished in Detroit, the architect acquired as many Bedford (Indiana) limestone blocks as he needed. They were smoothed somewhat to resemble Cotswold stone and produced masonry walls nine to twelve inches thick. A slate roof features copper gutters and downspouts at its edge. It is not a large house but is built on such an elegant scale that it seems to have been created for an English squire, a role that the new owner will undoubtedly accept.

Solid white oak was chosen for the woodwork inside, including the flooring. Original wallpapers remain in the downstairs bedroom and dining room, both—intended or not—in a late Arts and Crafts mode. These and other features make the walls excellent backdrops for the owner's Arts and Crafts collection, some of the pieces by Michigan designers.

Equally remarkable are the grounds, an especially appropriate circumstance because the new owner is a landscape architect. Originally the house was built on a lordly manor of forty acres. Today the manor has shrunk to two acres, mostly covered with a beech, maple, and hickory forest where a variety of violets, anemones, wild geraniums, trilliums, wild phlox, columbine, buttercups, and other Michigan wildflowers abound. An English touch is a myriad of daffodils planted shortly after the house was built. Close to the house are the remains of the formal gardens laid out by Edward H. Laird of Detroit in 1940. They are enclosed by yew and spruce hedges and are awaiting certain restoration.

With its formal garden hedges, Biddestone is a cottage one might happen upon in England's Cotswold district—but it was set down instead not far from Detroit. The trees help convey a sense of what the manor once encompassed.

Above: The house's architect, Marcus Burrowes, was a master at assembling architectural elements in a pleasing asymmetry, making his buildings look good from all vantage points.

Left: Original wallpaper in the dining room creates a fine backdrop for a Lifetime sideboard, a Come-Packt table with a Teco jardiniere, Gustav Stickley chairs, and an Edward Curtis print of the Cañon de Chelly.

Above: The nine-drawer chest in the bedroom was manufactured by Gustav Stickley's company, and Michael Adams designed the lamp. Everywhere are first editions of L. Frank Baum's *Wizard of Oz* stories.

Right: With its assembly of Rookwood and Marblehead vases, a limestone fireplace dominates the living room. The library table is from Charles P. Limbert, while the other pieces come from the Sticklets.

Opposite: In the study is an array of Weller, Teco, and Rookwood pottery. Lifetime made the trestle table. Behind it are an armchair and a bookcase from Gustav Stickley.

IN THE GREENE STYLE

A latecomer to the bungalow scene, this house was built in Pasadena in 1980—just as acres of bungalows in the Los Angeles area were being destroyed by intrusions of apartment houses and condominiums. Suddenly, following a pattern that began a generation earlier with the revival of interest in Victorian architecture, some people realized that a way of life was disappearing, one based on the old American love of the freestanding, single-family dwelling surrounded by a garden. These enthusiasts, many of them Arts and Crafts aficionados, began to buy bungalows, fight the intrusions, and in some cases—in Pasadena's "bungalow heaven," for example—save blocks of bungalows. At the same time they developed a community spirit that once characterized small-town America.

The almost inevitable next step was to build new bungalows. Although by the 1920s the term *bungalow* was often used derisively with connotations of too-small, unsophisticated, and quaint, the type did not die out. After World War II it reappeared in the Cape Cod cottage, Lustron houses, miles of tract housing in such places as Levittown on Long Island, and the ranch houses of California designers such as Cliff May. But by the 1980s the architects of one-story (often split-level) houses began to own up to their roots and finally admit that they were creating bungalows.

Opposite: This modern interpretation of the bungalow has no problem with hallways or, for that matter, skylights. There is no need for any bungalow to be dark.

Below: The sideboard in the dining room resembles the one in Greene and Greene's Gamble house. The dining set, however, is a reproduction of one by Charles Rennie Mackintosh.

This house salutes the bungalow revival. Its Arts and Crafts connection is clear: fine craftsmanship is immediately apparent. In this case the obvious influence on the architect, Lee Hershberger, was the work of the best of Pasadena's turn-of-the-century Arts and Crafts architects, Charles and Henry Greene. Hershberger is a long-time admirer of the Greenes' famous Gamble house (1909), and his wife served as executive secretary to the director. Rodger Whipple, the contractor and cabinetry designer, similarly had studied the Greenes' work since childhood. And the original owners, Martha and Peter Fitzpatrick, were equally taken with the Greenes' architecture, Martha having grown up in the 1904 house in South Pasadena they designed for Mrs. James A. Garfield, the widow of the assassinated president.

The Greene brothers' now-lost Bandini house (1903) in Pasadena was the intentional inspiration for the patio. Its squared-off columns placed around a central court recall an adobe house of old California.

Unlike Greene and Greene houses, the front door here is hidden away amid foliage and shadows. The pattern seen in the glass panel is a natural reflection rather than art glass—a serendipitous effect the Greenes missed out on using.

In spite of the attention given to the Greenes' "ultimate bungalows," however, they almost never designed one- or one-and-a-half-story houses. But here in this beautiful bungalow is the same immaculate attention to detail once bestowed on the well-to-do or the exceedingly wealthy, the Greenes' usual clients. It is in the Greene style, pared down for people of lesser means.

The present owners are obviously proud of their purchase from the Fitzpatricks. They have furnished the house with some Arts and Crafts pieces, such as the Mackintosh chairs in the dining room, but they are equally fond of contemporary art, which takes well to a house of wood and plaster.

Above: Aggressively masculine fireplaces are a familiar feature in bungalows old and new. Like bungalows built early in the century, the rough stone fireplace here continues to spell out a domestic ideal for home and family. The asymmetrical mantels add a modern signature.

Opposite: An alcove in the living room could have been inspired by Arthur S. and Alfred Heineman's "Home, Sweet Bungalow," shown on pages 118–19, except that this one is a library and not a "smokery." Librarians would not like the southern light, but it is a good place to read.

BUNGALOW BAZAAR

Old bungalows are being acquired today by people who are well aware of the intrinsic style and historical significance of these houses. They want their furnishings to reflect that style, even if the original owners could not. Arts and Crafts furnishings look right in many of these bungalows simply because so many Arts and Crafts examples were built. Bungalow enthusiasts consequently are choosing Limbert tables, Stickley chairs, Van Erp lamps, and Morris patterns to furnish their homes in style.

Authentic reproductions and thoughtful adaptations are keeping pace with the demand, as the furnishings in the following catalogue show. The items were chosen as examples that suit the period from 1900 to 1920. Arts and Crafts lovers have a multitude of furnishings to choose from; those with Spanish, Colonial Revival, Tudor, and Moderne houses less so. In such cases, antiques stores remain a good stop. Many more items are available from the suppliers listed. Just remember that you have to live with your furnishings. The best advice is to make your bungalow a part of your own biography.

Prairie Spindle Chair

Quartersawn white oak or cherry. 29½″ high, 42½″ wide, 37½″ deep. No. 89-417 or 91-417. L. and J. G. Stickley.
This chair with corbeled arms and leather or fabric cushions (below) features Craftsman elements—the graceful, slender vertical lines of the spindle construction and the low, horizontal appearance of the Prairie Style.

Prairie Settle

Quartersawn white oak or cherry. 29″ high, 84½″ wide, 37½″ deep. No. 89-220 or 91-220. L. and J. G. Stickley.
Leopold Stickley designed this settle (below right) to complement the long, low lines of Prairie Style houses. To emphasize its horizontal appearance, the settle extends beyond its vertical supports with corbeled arms, a popular feature of Prairie furnishings.

Arts and Crafts Love Seat

Honduras mahogany. 35″ high, 68″ wide, 37″ deep. Berkeley Mills.
Although usually constructed of mahogany, this arched love seat (center right) was inspired by the oak Arts and Crafts pieces that appeared around the beginning of the twentieth century. It is available in a variety of woods and comes with goose-down cushions and two throw pillows.

Prairie Settle

Solid quartersawn white oak. Variety of finishes from light yellow ocher to dark brown. 29″ high, 84″ wide, 37″ deep. Warren Hile Studio.
Both Gustav Stickley and Frank Lloyd Wright created chairs and sofas with spindles on the back and sides. This leather-cushioned settle (above left), paired with a trestle table, recalls the designs created for Prairie houses.

Spindle Settle

Quartersawn white oak or cherry. 49″ high, 48½″ wide, 24½″ deep, 26½″ arm height. No. 89-286 or 91-286. L. and J. G. Stickley.
The early catalogues for Gustav Stickley's furniture touted the spindle design as decorative yet structurally simple. This settle (left) recreates Stickley's original Arts and Crafts design featuring a tall back.

Morris Chair

Cherry or quartersawn white oak with faceted ebony pegs. 43″ high, 32″ wide, 39″ deep. Mack and Rodel Cabinetmakers.

The British Arts and Crafts leader William Morris is perhaps best known for his Morris chair. This version (below) has laced leather cushions and, like all Morris chairs, an adjustable back and broad arms.

Greene and Greene–Style Rocker

Mahogany with ebony inlay. 42″ high, 26½″ wide, 37″ deep. David B. Hellman Studio.

This custom-made rocker (below) is fashioned after one in Greene and Greene's Gamble house (1909) in Pasadena, California. Charles Greene produced most of the firm's furniture designs, often working with the furniture craftsmen Peter and John Hall.

Ellis Rocker

Quartersawn white oak. 43″ high, 25″ wide, 31½″ deep. No. 89-353½R. L. and J. G. Stickley

The architect Harvey Ellis briefly worked for Gustav Stickley in 1903, designing furniture and illustrations for Stickley's The Craftsman. A copy of one of his rockers (below) is available in oak or cherry with or without an inlay.

Coonley Chair

Cherry or beech. 37″ high, 16⅞″ wide, 18½″ deep. Cassina/FLW Foundation.

Slat-back chairs (above) appear often in Frank Lloyd Wright's interior designs.

Robie Chair

Cherry or beech. 52½″ high, 15¾″ wide, 18″ deep. Cassina/FLW Foundation.

Wright's tall-back chairs (right) are suited to large Prairie bungalows.

Reader's Side Chair

Solid oil-finished cherry. Full-grain leather seat in various colors or custom fabric. 44″ high, 20″ wide, 19″ deep. No. RSC. Thos. Moser Cabinetmakers.

Appropriate for libraries, offices, and dining rooms, this slat-back Arts and Crafts chair (above) appears simple but is constructed using complex mortise-and-tenon joints.

Limbert Tabouret

Fumed quartersawn white oak. 26″ high, 16″ diameter. Mack and Rodel Cabinetmakers.
This small table (below) is copied from a design in the 1905 Charles P. Limbert Company catalogue. Limbert, an American, produced popular Mission furniture that imitated Continental designers such as Charles Rennie Mackintosh and C.F.A. Voysey.

Stickley Library Table

Quartersawn white oak. Leather and nail-head top shown. 29½″ high, 42″ or 48″ diameter. No. 89-407 LT. L. and J. G. Stickley
Designed by Gustav Stickley in 1903, this commemorative piece (below) was reissued fifty years after his death. It first appeared in the May 1903 issue of The Craftsman *and features canted legs and keyed tenons.*

Limbert Double Oval Table

Fumed quartersawn white oak. 29″ high, 48″ diameter. Paul Kemner.
A classic Limbert design, this double oval (top right) has rectangular cutouts.

Allen Table

Cherry or beech. 27¾″ high, 101¼″ long, 41¾″ wide. Cassina/FLW Foundation.
A 1917 Wright design (center right), this table suits spacious Prairie bungalows.

Greene Fern Table

Mahogany. Marble top. Kit. 16″–36″ high. *American Bungalow* magazine.
Precut kits based on a Gamble house design come ready to assemble.

Prairie Table

Maple. Inlay or glass top. 30″ high, 84″ long, 38″ wide. Berkeley Mills.
Tall slat-back chairs can accompany this Wrightian table for eight (right).

Trestle Desk

Solid quartersawn white oak. Variety of finishes from light yellow ocher to dark brown. 29″ high, 54″ long, 32″ deep. Warren Hile Studio. *Simple and functional, this desk embodies the philosophy of the Arts and Crafts movement, which favored utilitarian furnishings with a hand-crafted look. Its finish uses century-old methods and materials.*

Dining Room Table and Chairs

Solid quartersawn white oak. Variety of finishes from light yellow ocher to dark brown. Table: 29″ high, 78″ long, 38″ wide. Chairs: 42½″ high, 19″ wide, 22″ deep. Warren Hile Studio. *Inspired by Gustav Stickley, the table resembles his director's table, while the chairs feature wraparound leather seats with copper tacks.*

New Century Book Table

Solid oil-finished cherry. 29" high, 32" square. No. NC-BT. Thos. Moser Cabinetmakers.

This bookcase, modeled after a Stickley design, includes 8½ lineal feet of storage on all four sides. It can accommodate books up to 10⅞" high by 10" deep. The New Century series, which features vertical-slat construction, includes companion pieces.

"Kaidan" (Staircase) Tansu

Mahogany. 72" high, 72" wide, 20" deep. Berkeley Mills.
Inspired by modular oriental boxes, these stacking chests have a Japanese feel. Although not designed as a staircase, the solid construction makes them structurally sound enough to walk on.

Ellis Bookcase

Quartersawn white oak. Handleaded glass panels. Variety of finishes from light yellow ocher to dark brown. 58" high, 46" wide, 13" deep. Warren Hile Studio.

This handsome bookcase is modeled after a popular design by Harvey Ellis, who worked for Gustav Stickley to produce refined furniture inspired by innovative European designers.

Ellis Tall Chest

Quartersawn white oak. 55½" high, 38" wide, 20" deep. No. 89-913. L. and J. G. Stickley.

Designed by Harvey Ellis, this chest of drawers is less bulky than other Mission oak pieces. It has tapered posts, blind dovetailed crossrails, and solid cast-copper hardware. The chest is part of a Mission-style bedroom suite that includes matching pieces.

Fall-Front Desk and Drawers

Quartersawn white oak. 44½" high, 36½" wide, 15" deep. No. 89-1729. L. and J. G. Stickley.

A Gustav Stickley design introduced in 1905, this features pinned-dowel joints, through tenons, and copper hardware. The desk includes a central compartment with a panel door, nine letter compartments, and two vertical document compartments.

Ellis Secretary

Quartersawn oak. 58″ high, 49″ wide, 16″ deep. Warren Hile Studio.

With its handleaded glass panels and handwrought copper hardware, this large cabinet (below) is fashioned after a turn-of-the-century Harvey Ellis design. For a brief period Ellis enhanced the plainer Stickley furniture pieces with subtle markings and metal inlays.

Craftsman Sideboard

Cherry shown. 30″ high, 80″ wide, 20″ deep. Berkeley Mills.

Merging oriental lines with the Arts and Crafts philosophy that good design follows function and materials, this simple, utilitarian piece (below right) recalls the work of Craftsman leaders from William Morris and Gustav Stickley to Frank Lloyd Wright and the Greene brothers.

Greene Sideboard

Mahogany, ebony, and inlays of mother-of-pearl. 36″ high, 79″ wide, 24″ deep. James-Randell Reproductions/Ipekjian Custom Woodwork.

This sideboard (center right) is a reproduction of Charles Greene's design for the Thorsen house (1909) in Berkeley, California. With its inlays and oriental influences, it was one of Greene's most elegant creations.

Chafing Dish Cabinet

Oak or cherry. 40″ high, 32″ wide, 19″ deep. No. 89-55 or 91-55. L. and J. G. Stickley.

A reissue of a design produced by the Roycroft Colony in East Aurora, New York, this cabinet (above) replicates one of only three known originals. It features a locking door, an adjustable shelf, and leaded glass on all sides. Interior lights are optional.

Glasgow Sideboard

Cherry with maple inlay shown. Copper door pulls. 46″ high, 70″ wide, 22″ deep. Mack and Rodel Cabinetmakers.

Influenced by the work of the Scottish designer Charles Rennie Mackintosh, this sideboard (left) is constructed with adjustable interior shelving and can serve as a linen or china cabinet. Custom interiors are available.

China Bed

Oil-finished cherry. Full to king.
Thos. Moser Cabinetmakers.
*This bed (right) was inspired by the
intersecting lines of oriental designs.*

Cheval Mirror

Oak or cherry. 62″ high, 26″ wide,
16″ deep. L. and J. G. Stickley.
*This Gustav Stickley reproduction
mirror (bottom left) dates to 1904.*

Roycroft Magazine Pedestal

Oak or cherry. 63½″ high, 18″ wide,
18″ deep. L. and J. G. Stickley.
*This reissued bookcase (bottom
center) is a classic Roycroft design.*

Tall Case Clock

Oak or cherry. 80″ high, 27″ wide,
16″ deep. L. and J. G. Stickley.
*A solid brass etched dial enhances
this 1910 reproduction (bottom right).*

Prairie Bed

Oak. Twin to California king. Headboard: 52″ high. Warren Hile Studio. *The bed's spindled head- and footboards recall Prairie Style designs.*

Folding Screen with Leather Inserts

Fumed quartersawn white oak. 68″ high, 66″ wide. Paul Kemner. *This screen features fine joinery in a bold Arts and Crafts style.*

Double Costumer Hat Rack

Oak or cherry. 72″ high, 24″ wide, 20½″ deep. L. and J. G. Stickley. *Leopold Stickley designed this simple hat rack with brass hooks.*

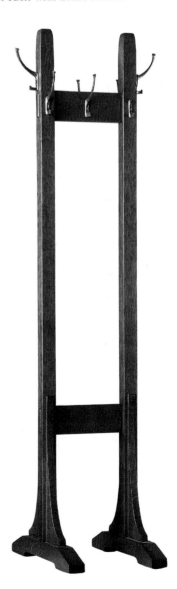

Huntington Hanging Pendant

Hanging light. Brass, antique brass finish. Gold-white iridescent art glass. Various heights: 32"–42," widths: 14"–18." No. HCM-18WO-AB. Arroyo Craftsman.

Modeled after the designs of Frank Lloyd Wright and Prairie School architecture, this light is appropriate for vaulted ceilings because of its special hanging assembly.

Evergreen Post Mount

Post light for gardens and pathways. Solid brass, bronze finish shown. White opalescent art glass. Various heights: 10¾"–19½," widths: 7"–16." No. EP-7A-WO-BZ. Arroyo Craftsman.

This exterior lantern sits atop a post and comes in varied metal finishes and glass as well as column, pendant, wall mount, and chandelier versions.

Mission Flush Wall Mount

Wall mount. Brass, verdigris patina finish. Gold-white iridescent art glass. Various heights: 7⅜"–12," widths: 6"–10," projections: 6"–10." No. MW-6GW. Arroyo Craftsman.

Inspired by California's popular Mission architecture, this exterior or interior light is also available as a Mission wall mount that is suspended from a gently curving arm.

Guest Room Sconce

Wall mount. Mahogany with ebony and teak details. Copper-foiled, iridescent stained glass. 24" high, 12" wide, 14" projection. Sundance Studios.

A replica of the original sconces in the guest bedroom of the 1909 Gamble house in Pasadena, California, this wall light is one of a series of increasingly inventive lighting fixtures found in Greene and Greene houses.

Cottage Grove Sconce

Three-light wall mount. Polished nickel finish shown. Interior satin-etched glass shade. 9" high, 17" wide, 9" projection. No. W977. Rejuvenation Lamp and Fixture Company.

Early-twentieth-century Mission-style lamps inspired this series of fixtures, whose square, simple shape reflects Arts and Crafts ideals.

Sherwood Sconce

Wall mount. Antique brass finish shown. Handblown art glass shade from Lundberg Studios. 11" high, 5" wide, 7" projection. No. W300. Rejuvenation Lamp and Fixture Company.

Transitional in style, this sconce displays turn-of-the-century influences, among them Art Nouveau and the work of Louis C. Tiffany.

Ellis Round Sconce
Wall mount. Copper. 4″ diameter.
No. 126. Aurora Studios.
A Harvey Ellis design, the original
of this replica dates to about 1903.

Castle Gate Lantern
Solid brass. 5″ wide, 11″ shown.
No. 818-5-CH. Brass Light Gallery.
This exterior lantern comes in various
sizes, mounts, and glass options.

Greene Wall Sconce
Wall mount. Copper. 12″ high,
6″ square, roof 11¼.″ Buffalo Studios.
A Greene and Greene design inspired
this Arts and Crafts light.

Berkeley Free-Hanging Pendant
Hanging light. Brass, antique
brass finish. Frosted glass with a
pine design. Various heights:
10⅛″–14¼,″ diameters: 5⅝″–8⅜.″
No. BH-7FPF-AB. Arroyo Craftsman.
Based on the designs of Gustav
Stickley and Dirk Van Erp, this
interior or exterior lamp is available
in three sizes. The frosted glass
shown here is optional.

Stamford Lantern
Wall mount. Solid brass. Verdigris
patina finish shown. Gold-white
art glass. Various heights: 7″–10,″
widths: 7″–9,″ projections: 9″–11.″
No. 764-7-SAW. Brass Light Gallery.
The Stamford is a classic interior or
exterior lantern design with a cross-
bow pattern from 1910, reintroduced
and available in three sizes and a
variety of mounting styles.

San Simeon Wall Arm
Wall mount. Solid brass. 12″ high,
7″ wide, 12″ projection. No. WA280-7.
Rockscapes.
Suitable for Spanish Colonial Revival
houses, this lamp is available in a
variety of lacquered finishes and
glass-panel options. Its inspiration was
the eclectic castle (1919–37) designed
for William Randolph Hearst along
the California coast.

Oak Tree Lamps

Wall-mount sconces and hanging light. Steel and mica, rust finish. Sconces: 8¾" high, 7" wide, 3⅞" projection. Hanging lamp: 46" long, 15½" diameter, 10" high lamp body. Omega Too.

An Arts and Crafts–style oak-tree motif enriches these interior lamps. The hanging light has a handwrought canopy, chain, and body.

Fifth Avenue Hanging Light

Single-chain hanging light. Polished brass finish. Satin opal-etched glass shade. Various lengths: 26"–38," 17" diameter. No. C912. Rejuvenation Lamp and Fixture Company.

Appropriate for early-twentieth-century Colonial Revival bungalows, the style's popularity coincided with American interest in its eighteenth-century heritage.

East Bank Flush Ceiling Fixture

Ceiling light with bowl shade. Polished brass finish shown. Exterior satin-etched glass shade. 9" high, 16" diameter. No. C609. Rejuvenation Lamp and Fixture Company.

Featuring subtle ornament, this typical turn-of-the-century fixture is designed for low ceilings. It reflects an amalgam of styles, from Georgian to Colonial Revival.

Raymond Four-Light Chandelier

Hanging light. Brass, polished-brass finish. White opalescent art glass or amber mica panels. 35⅞" or 37¼" high, 23⅞" wide, 9" fixture height. No. RCH-6/4WO-PB. Arroyo Craftsman.

This light is one in a series named after the Raymond Hotel in Pasadena, California. The handworked brass is reminiscent of the Craftsman spirit.

Hawthorne Hanging Light

Hanging light. Solid brass, verde antique finish shown. Cream art glass. Various heights: 14"–21," 17" diameter, 8" ceiling canopy. No. C222. Rejuvenation Lamp and Fixture Company.

An indoor or outdoor lamp available in a variety of finishes, this classic Arts and Crafts–style fixture is supplied with a solid brass chain.

Sun Panel Flush Ceiling Fixture

Ceiling light. Satin antique brass finish shown. Sandblasted-frost art glass. 12" wide, 7" deep shown. No. 811-12-FCH. Brass Light Gallery.

Available in larger sizes, this flush ceiling light is suited to hallways, bedrooms, and other interior spaces. The overlays on the glass panels are in geometric patterns, reflecting the lamp's Prairie Style–inspired design.

Round Bean-Pot Lamp

Table lamp. Hammered copper. Mica shade. 12″ high, 11″ diameter. No. 804. Aurora Studios.

This mushroom-style table lamp with one socket is a replica of a Dirk Van Erp original created about 1915. Its design was immensely popular in the Craftsman era, making bean-pot lamps a staple of well-decorated Arts and Crafts homes.

Oakland Lamp

Table lamp. Solid copper, mottled copper finish. Mica shade. 17″ high, 14″ diameter. No. T420. Rejuvenation Lamp and Fixture Company.

A copy of another Dirk Van Erp lamp from about 1912, this distinctive trumpet-shaped version bears his typical deeply sloped shade—a form recalling the overhanging roofs of the bungalows in which they were placed.

Stickley Floor Lamp

Standing light with post and lantern. Oak and copper stand. Hammered-copper and mica shade. 60″ high. No. 401. Aurora Studios.

Adapted from a Gustav Stickley original dated about 1907, this floor lamp's mica shade is modified from the actual willow shade that Stickley used and shows the influence of Dirk Van Erp's designs.

Prairie Table Lamp

Table lamp. Various finishes and art glasses. 18″ high. No. 802-8-CB. Brass Light Gallery.

Inspired by designs created by Frank Lloyd Wright and other architects of the Prairie School, the Prairie series of lamps is available with several shade overlays. The table lamp shown here has an Arts and Crafts–style crossbow overlay.

Junior Rivet Lamp

Table lamp. Hammered copper. Mica shade. 17″ diameter. No. 806. Aurora Studios.

Another replica from the noted Arts and Crafts designer Dirk Van Erp, this lamp has four sockets and a traditional rivet design. The original dates to 1911. Van Erp was a Dutch-born California metal artisan who specialized in hammered-copper lamps.

Morris Ceiling Paper

Wallpaper. Handprinted. 21″ wide, 21″ repeat, 7 yds. per roll. No. WP81236. Scalamandré.

The original pattern for this design was created by William Morris and called "The Wreath." Devised to create all-over pattern in a room, it dates to around 1883 and was reproduced for the North American Branch of the William Morris Society.

Pimpernel Wallpaper

Wallpaper. Handprinted. 21½″ wide, 16 ¹³⁄₁₆″ repeat, 7 yds. per roll. No. WP81226-001. Scalamandré.

This subtle, monochromatic paper was designed by William Morris and first printed in England in 1876 by Morris and Company. The stylized floral motif was a favorite of Morris's and was frequently imitated by his design contemporaries.

Broad Meadows Wallpaper

Wallpaper. 21″ wide, 14″ repeat, 7 yds. per roll. Various colorways. Waterhouse Wallhangings.

The original for this pattern was found in the entrance hall of a Berkshire cottage known as Broad Meadows. It is possibly a William Morris design, manufactured by Jeffrey and Company. This reproduction is machine made.

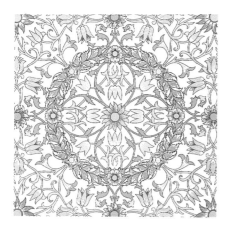

Trellis Wallpaper

Wallpaper. 21″ wide, 21″ repeat, 11 yds. per roll. No. 157. Morris and Company by Sanderson.

Designed in 1862 by William Morris for Morris and Company, this pattern is an early example of the decorative style that made Morris famous. Its subtle floral and bird design was created to lend a quiet, natural backdrop to Craftsman houses.

Golden Lily Wallpaper

Wallpaper. 21″ wide, 17½″ repeat, 11 yds. per roll. No. 356. Morris and Company by Sanderson.

Designed by John Henry Dearle in 1899, this paper was a Morris and Company pattern printed by Jeffrey and Company. Dearle was one of the many artists and designers who worked for the English Arts and Crafts leader William Morris.

Honeysuckle Wallpaper

Wallpaper. Handscreened. 27″ wide, 15½″ repeat, 5 yds. per roll. Bradbury and Bradbury.

Available in three color schemes (see this book's cover and endpapers), this English floral pattern dates to around 1910. The palette shown above and on the endpapers features olive, khaki, ocher, and leaf green—natural tones favored by Craftsman designers.

Briar Rose Wallpaper

Wallpaper. Handscreened. 27″ wide, 9″ repeat, 5 yds. per roll. Bradbury and Bradbury.

The 1901 rose pattern (below) was adapted from a design by the British architect C.F.A. Voysey, who was also renowned for his furniture. Voysey believed that wallpaper patterns should be inconspicuous, two-dimensional reflections of natural images.

Oak Leaf Frieze

Wallpaper. Handscreened. 27″ repeat. Bradbury and Bradbury.

Adapted from a pattern found in an Arts and Crafts house in Los Angeles, this frieze (left) was the work of an anonymous American designer in 1910. It blends Craftsman and modernist styles, using a natural theme and muted colors with geometric designs and a bright purple.

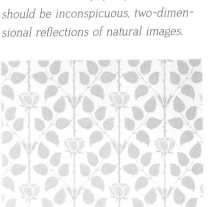

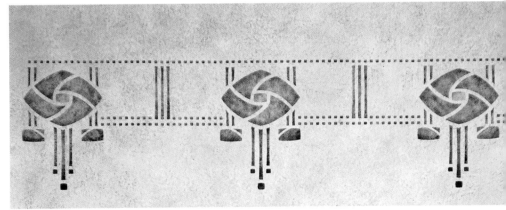

Stag Wallpaper

Wallpaper. Handscreened. 21″ wide, 21¼″ repeat, 6 yds. per roll. J. R. Burrows and Company.

This C.F.A. Voysey pattern (above) was published in The Studio *in 1896 and depicts an abstracted version of an English royal park. The pattern was later revised for textiles and carpets, although this is a hand-silkscreened version of the original wallpaper.*

Wisteria Frieze

Wall stencil. Acrylic and oil-based paints. 9½″ high, 20″ wide. Helen Foster Stencils.

Arts and Crafts stencils appropriate for bungalows often featured soft colors and provided a quiet background to complement the rustic furniture found in Craftsman homes. Stylized versions of vines, stems, and branches were popular (center right).

Rose Frieze

Wall stencil. Acrylic and oil-based paints. 7½″–10¾″ high, 11¾″–16¾″ wide. Helen Foster Stencils.

The flat appearance of stencils, which appealed to Arts and Crafts advocates, provided an inexpensive decorating scheme for bungalows. This geometric rose design (above right) uses an abstract floral motif that was a favorite of Charles Rennie Mackintosh.

Fir Tree Frieze

Wallpaper. Handscreened. 13½″ high, 27″ repeat. Bradbury and Bradbury. *Although many designers scorned elaborate wall coverings, friezes were often used to decorate plain papered walls or wood paneling. This pattern (top) was created by an English designer around 1911. The forest motif, modeled after Walter Crane's "May Tree Frieze," was common.*

River Frieze

Wallpaper. Handscreened. 11″ high, 20½″ repeat. Bradbury and Bradbury. *Arts and Crafts landscape friezes became popular between 1900 and 1920. The original of this anonymous frieze (center) is dated around 1910. Typical for the Craftsman era, it uses subdued, woodsy colors and a peaceful pictorial design to create a calming atmosphere.*

Woodland Frieze

Wall stencil. Acrylic and oil-based paints. 10″ high, 26½″ repeat. Helen Foster Stencils. *The familiar theme of woodland designs extended to friezes that sometimes were used to fill the space above high wainscoting, such as this version (above), featuring a rich leaf-green color. Stencils added polish to otherwise plain walls.*

Lion and Dove Frieze

Wallpaper. Handscreened. 26½″ wide, 46″ repeat. Bradbury and Bradbury. *Created by the English Arts and Crafts designer Walter Crane and originally manufactured by Jeffrey and Company, this pattern (left) was first printed in 1900 and displayed at the Paris Exhibition. The "Wilderness shall blossom" theme is taken from Isaiah in the Old Testament.*

Apple Tree Frieze

Wallpaper. Handscreened. 13½″ wide, 21″ repeat. Bradbury and Bradbury. *Pendant friezes appeared often in early-twentieth-century interior designs. This frieze (left) is adapted from an American design dated 1915. The geometric shapes reflect the influences of Europeans such as Charles Rennie Mackintosh and the Vienna Secessionist Josef Hoffmann.*

River Scene

Gouache. Framed: 20″ high, 17″ wide. Anita Munman Design. *An 1895 lithograph by Arthur Wesley Dow inspired this view (above).*

Tall Gingko

Gouache. Framed: 26½″ high, 14½″ wide. Anita Munman Design. *Gingko images (left) appeared often in Arts and Crafts designs.*

Tall Trees

Gouache. Framed: 23¾″ high, 18″ wide. Anita Munman Design. *This original painting (above) was inspired by Dard Hunter.*

American Beauty Pillow

Linen with hand embroidery and hand stenciling. 20″ square. Dianne Ayres Arts and Crafts Period Textiles. *The rose is a common motif of the Arts and Crafts period. This pillow adapts a design offered around 1910 as an embroidery kit from H. E. Verran Company. Available as a kit or completed. Coordinating curtains may be custom ordered.*

Ginkgo Pillow

Imported European linen with hand embroidery and appliqué. 22″ wide, 15″ high. United Crafts. *The ginkgo-leaf design was first produced by Gustav Stickley's Craftsman Workshops and was frequently used on textiles. Two decorative faux-shell buttons adorn the opening in the back of this pillow. Feather-pillow inserts are available.*

Seed Pod Wall Hanging

Linen with hand embroidery and appliqué. 29″ wide, 41″ long. Dianne Ayres Arts and Crafts Period Textiles. *Gustav Stickley's Craftsman Workshops originally offered this design as door curtains.*

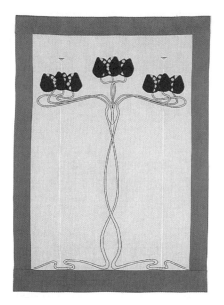

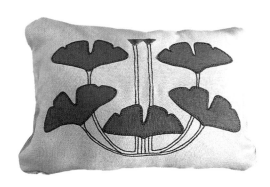

Meadow Lily Lace Curtains

95% cotton, 5% polyester. Various lengths. J. R. Burrows and Company. *This American Arts and Crafts design, made in Scotland, dates to around 1910 and was originally advertised in the 1911 and 1912 catalogues of the Come-Packt Furniture Company in Ann Arbor, Michigan. Craftsman windows were usually either left plain or covered with light, simple fabrics.*

Sue Ellen's Lily Curtains

Imported Irish linen, cotton, or silk. Lined or unlined. Lily motif: 15″ high, 3³⁄₄″ wide. Custom made for various window frames. Ann Wallace and Friends. *This appliquéd lily motif is available in three styles—vertical, corner, or medallion—and a variety of colors. The design adapts easily to most window sizes.*

China Tree Table Scarf

Imported European linen with hand embroidery and appliqué. 66,″ 76,″ or 96″ long, 18″ wide. United Crafts. *Embroidery satisfied the Arts and Crafts desire to return to handicrafts of an earlier age. Fashioned after period designs, this table scarf can be used on tables, sideboards, and dressers. Napkins in the same motif with handrolled hems are also available.*

Loddon Fabric

100% cotton. Handprinted.
48″ wide, 19 ³⁄₁₆″ repeat. No. 6802.
Scalamandré.

This intricate, swirling floral pattern from 1884 epitomizes William Morris's popular decorative style. Despite his desire to promote good design, his handprinted textiles were expensive and thus not widely available to everyone.

Mede Rug

Handknotted wool. Various sizes:
4′ by 6′ to 10′ by 14.′ Nature's Loom.
A medieval influence can be seen in this Morris-inspired design.

Bloomsbury Rug

Handknotted wool. Various sizes:
4′ by 6′ to 10′ by 14.′ Nature's Loom.
This pattern is adapted from "The Fintona," a design by C.F.A. Voysey.

Strawberry Thief Fabric

100% cotton. Handprinted. 49″ wide,
19 ⁷⁄₁₆″ repeat. No. 6792. Scalamandré.
This 1883 original William Morris design was the first successful indigo discharge printing at Merton Abbey. Morris used birds and even rabbits in some of his designs, but he did not think that he was skilled at depicting birds and usually deferred to his other designers for them.

Vine and Pomegranate Carpet

Three-ply ingrain carpet. 36″ wide,
16″ repeat. J. R. Burrows and Company.
An authenticated reproduction of a design attributed to Kate Faulkner, who was an associate of William Morris, this pattern is available for use as upholstery or draperies as well as carpeting. The deep red and off-white color scheme is suited to many Victorian and Craftsman houses.

Tulip and Lily Carpet

Wilton carpet. 80% worsted wool,
20% nylon. 27″ wide, 10″ repeat.
Runner available. J. R. Burrows and Company.
This William Morris and Company design was developed around the 1870s. The Wilton method of creating carpets also produced power-loomed imitations of oriental rugs, which were popular for interiors of the period.

Arts and Crafts Tile

Handcrafted stoneware tile. Vasekraft glazes in various colors. Various sizes: 3″–8″ square. Fulper Tile.

Simple Arts and Crafts tiles such as these replaced the heavily decorated style of Victorian interior design. These are shown on a custom-designed fireplace, but they are also suitable for walls, hearths, countertops, and flooring.

Fulper Fireplace Tile

Handcrafted stoneware tile. Vasekraft glazes in various colors. Various sizes: 3″–8″ square. Fulper Tile.

A handpainted frieze is used with glazed tiles on this fireplace. The glaze formulas were developed in 1909 by William Hill Fulper II, who produced stoneware art pottery. Like many of his contemporaries, Fulper aimed to mix art and functionality.

Rosette and Leaves Tile

Clay tile. Creamy white satin-matte glaze. 4″ square. Winters Tileworks.

The rosette is an adaptation of stylized geometric roses that appeared around 1900 in the work of the Scottish interior designer Charles Rennie Mackintosh and the Art Nouveau designer Maurice Verneuil. The accompanying leaves are an original design added to the rose motif.

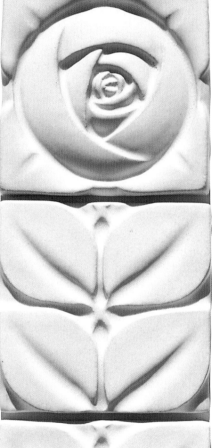

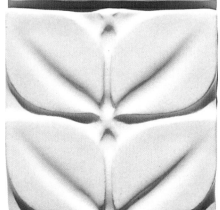

Persian Revival Tile Border

Ceramic tile. Handpainted on faience stoneware. 6″ high, 12″ wide (one-half detail shown). No. PR-1. Designs in Tile.

Hispano-Moresque styles were popular with California art tile studios in the early twentieth century. The tiles are created using the cuerda seca *technique of painting and glazing to give them an embossed quality.*

Calla Lily Tile

Molded clay. Handcrafted. 7⅝″ square. Available in various custom glazes. No. 88-122. The Meredith Collection.

This tile is an original design combining influences from the Arts and Crafts and Art Nouveau movements. Made from handcarved molds and nineteenth-century presses, these tiles are high-fired for durability.

Crane Tile

Ceramic tile. 18″ high, 6″ wide.
No. DM-1. Designs in Tile.
An adaptation of a William De Morgan design dating from around 1888, the swirling lines of the bird and foliage in this three-tile panel give the pattern an Art Nouveau quality. The tiles were glazed using the cuerda seca *coloring technique to produce an embossed appearance.*

Iris Tile

Molded clay. Available in various matte and gloss glaze colors.
4″ square. Winters Tileworks.
This design is an original inspired by the Arts and Crafts aesthetic and the popularity of floral motifs. Handmade and pounded into plaster press-molds, the tiles are crafted using the same techniques as those of early-twentieth-century artisans.

Carnation Tile

Ceramic tile. Handpainted in under-glaze. Available in documentary or custom colorways. 6″ high, 12″ wide (one-half detail shown).
Designs in Tile.
"Carnation" was another pattern from the studio of the British designer William De Morgan. Handpainted designs are appropriate for walls, backsplashes, and fireplace surrounds.

Green Dog Tile

White stoneware. Low relief, matte glaze. 3″ square and 6″ square.
Motawi Tileworks.
A medieval tile located on the floor of an English abbey was the basis for this whimsical design. It was originally an encaustic tile created in two colors of clay, probably dark brown and buff. This glazed rendering is appropriate for bungalow styles.

Willow Tree Tile

Molded clay. Handcrafted. Available in various custom glazes. 7⅝″ square.
No. 88-116. The Meredith Collection.
This nature-based tree pattern was inspired by a 1915 plaque created by Anna Frances Simpson. The hammered-texture frame and trim pieces imitate metalworkers' patterns that were characteristic of the Arts and Crafts period.

Craftsman Mailbox

Solid brass, lacquered verdigris finish. White or green art glass. 10" high, 10" wide, 5" deep or 14" high, 14" wide, 5" deep. Rockscapes.
A companion for prevalent Arts and Crafts–style lanterns and sconces, this mailbox carries through the rectilinear forms favored by many of the era's designers, including Frank Lloyd Wright and his Prairie colleagues.

Curtain Rods

Wrought iron. Various finishes. ½" or ³⁄₈" round or ½" square. Omega Too.
Rods such as these were likely to be found in Spanish or Tudor-style houses. Custom made, they can be adjusted to fit any window size.

Styles available include a spiral finial shown at the top, a spear finial shown at the center, and a wiggle finial pictured at the bottom. Tapestries, embroidered curtains, or heavy linens were the textiles suggested as appropriate for these period revival rooms.

Stickley Drawer Pulls

Copper. Bookcase pull: 3⅝" high, 1¼" wide. Top drawer pull: 3⅛" wide. Bottom pull: 3⅝" wide. Buffalo Studios.
Shown here are a bookcase pull with a keyhole and two drawer pulls, all L. and J. G. Stickley designs. Arts and Crafts aficionados sought hand-hammered and handcrafted metalwork details for their homes and furnishings.

Greene and Greene Entry Door Handle and Lock Plate

Copper. 8½" high, 3¼" wide. Buffalo Studios.
This distinctive "cloud lift" door handle was designed by Charles and Henry Greene for the Gamble house. The outside set has a large hole plate and key lock, the inside set a T-turn plate. Both come with special rectangular and square screws.

Exterior Front Door Plate, Interior Front Door Plate, and Bell Plate

Copper with green glass. Exterior door plate: 21" high, 4" wide. Interior door plate: 14" high, 3½" wide. Bell plate: 5½" high, 2½" wide (⅝" hole). Buffalo Studios.
This hand-hammered pattern was popularized around 1910 by a California company. A patinated brass button is available for the door plates.

SUPPLIERS

Listed here are suppliers of items in the preceding catalogue as well as others who provide products that may be of interest to bungalow owners.

Acorn Manufacturing Company
P.O. Box 31
Mansfield, Mass. 02048
508-339-4500
800-835-0121

American Bungalow
P.O. Box 756
Sierra Madre, Calif. 91025-0756
818-355-3363
800-350-3363

Arroyo Craftsman Lighting
4509 Little John Street
Baldwin Park, Calif. 91706
818-960-9411

Arts and Crafts Mantel Clocks
P.O. Box 451
Northfield, N.Y. 13856
607-865-8372

V. Michael Ashford Design
6543 Alpine Drive, S.W.
Olympia, Wash. 98502
206-352-0694

Aurora Studios/
The Mission Oak Shop
50 Bull Hill Road
Woodstock, Conn. 06281
203-928-6662

Dianne Ayres Arts and Crafts
Period Textiles
5427 Telegraph Avenue
Suite W2
Oakland, Calif. 94609
510-654-1645

Ball and Ball Hardware Reproductions
463 West Lincoln Highway
Exton, Pa. 19341
215-363-7330

Berkeley Mills
East/West Design
2830 Seventh Street
Berkeley, Calif. 94710
510-549-2854

Bradbury and Bradbury
P.O. Box 155
Benicia, Calif. 94510
707-746-1900

Brass Light Gallery
131 South First Street
Milwaukee, Wis. 53204
414-271-8300

Buffalo Studios
1925 East Deere Avenue
Santa Ana, Calif. 92705
714-250-7333

J. R. Burrows and Company
P.O. Box 522
Rockland, Mass. 02370
617-982-1812

Cassina USA
200 McKay Road
Huntington Station, N.Y. 11746
516-423-4560

Crown City Hardware Company
1047 North Allen Avenue
Pasadena, Calif. 91104
818-794-1188

Designs in Tile
Box 358
Mount Shasta, Calif. 96067
916-926-5293

Fair Oak Workshops
P.O. Box 5578
River Forest, Ill. 60305
800-341-0597

Michael FitzSimmons Decorative Arts
311 West Superior Street
Chicago, Ill. 60610
312-787-0496

Helen Foster Stencils
71 Main Street
Sanford, Maine 04073
207-490-2625

Fulper Tile
P.O. Box 373
Yardley, Pa. 19067
215-736-8512

Green Design Furniture Company
267 Commercial Street
Portland, Maine 04101
207-775-4234

David B. Hellman Studio
86 Highland Avenue
Watertown, Mass. 02172
617-923-4829

Warren Hile Studio
89 East Montecito Avenue
Sierra Madre, Calif. 91024
818-355-4382

Holton Furniture and Frame
5515 Doyle Street
Suite 2
Emeryville, Calif. 94608
510-450-0350

James-Randell Reproductions
768 North Fair Oaks Avenue
Pasadena, Calif. 91103-3044
818-792-5025

Paul Kemner Furniture Craftsman
2829 Rockwood
Toledo, Ohio 43610-1625
419-241-8278

LeBlanc Furniture
2114 Western Avenue
Seattle, Wash. 98121
206-443-3876

Mack and Rodel
Cabinetmakers
44 Leighton Road
Pownal, Maine 04069
207-688-4483

Carol Mead Wallpapers
434 Deerfield Road
Pomfret, Conn. 06259
203-963-1927

Mica Lamp Company
520 State Street
Glendale, Calif. 91203
818-241-7227

Moravian Pottery and Tile Works
130 Swamp Road
Doylestown, Pa. 18901
215-345-6722

Thos. Moser Cabinetmakers
P.O. Box 1237
Auburn, Maine 04211
207-784-3332

Motawi Tileworks
33 North Staebler Road
Ann Arbor, Mich. 48103
313-213-0017

Anita Munman Design
729 South Carpenter Avenue
Oak Park, Ill. 60304
708-383-2884

Nature's Loom
32 East 31st Street
New York, N.Y. 10016
212-686-2002
800-365-2002

Omega Too
2204 San Pablo Avenue
Berkeley, Calif. 94702
510-843-3636

Pewabic Pottery
10125 East Jefferson Avenue
Detroit, Mich. 48214
313-822-0954

Pleasant Valley Pillow Company
301 South Old Stage Road
Mount Shasta, Calif. 96067
916-926-5293

Rejuvenation Lamp and Fixture
Company
1100 S.E. Grand Avenue
Portland, Ore. 97214
503-231-1900

Rockscapes
419 North Larchmont Boulevard
Suite 68
Los Angeles, Calif. 90004
213-469-3637
800-469-3637

Rogue River Studios
P.O. Box 91
Jacksonville, Ore. 97530
503-899-8106

Roy Electric Company
1054 Coney Island Avenue
Brooklyn, N.Y. 11230
800-366-3347

Roycroft Associates
31 South Grove Street
Aurora, N.Y. 14052
716-652-3333

Arthur Sanderson and Sons
979 Third Avenue
New York, N.Y. 10022
212-319-7220

Scalamandré
950 Third Avenue
New York, N.Y. 10022
212-980-3888
718-361-8500

Schumacher
939 Third Avenue
New York, N.Y. 10022
212-415-3900

L. and J. G. Stickley
P.O. Box 480
Manlius, N.Y. 13104-0480
315-682-5500

Sundance Studios
P.O. Box 1865
Arboles, Colo. 81121
970-883-5362

Thibaut Wallcoverings
480 Frelinghuysen Avenue
Newark, N.J. 07114
201-643-3777

Tile Restoration Center
3511 Interlake North
Seattle, Wash. 98103
206-633-4866

Tile Showcase
Boston Design Center
Suite 639
Boston, Mass. 02210
617-426-6515

United Crafts
127 West Putnam Avenue
Suite 123
Greenwich, Conn. 06830
203-869-4898

Ann Wallace and Friends
767 Linwood Avenue
St. Paul, Minn. 55105
612-228-9611

Waterhouse Wallhangings
99 Paul Sullivan Way
Boston, Mass. 02118
617-423-7688

Winters Tileworks
2547 Eighth Street
Suite 33
Berkeley, Calif. 94710
510-533-7624

Wood Classics
P.O. Box 4AB5
Gardiner, N.Y. 12525
914-255-5599

SOURCES OF INFORMATION

From tall case clocks to timepieces for walls and mantels, clocks were important components of well-furnished Arts and Crafts homes. This modern flat-top wall clock recalls the spare lines and natural woods used by the Stickleys and their contemporaries. Courtesy Thos. Moser Cabinetmakers.

Other than *American Bungalow*, no other periodical or organization specifically addresses historic bungalows alone. A number of general historical and historic preservation sources, however, have information and provide assistance that may be of help to bungalow owners and enthusiasts. Because so many remaining bungalows are Arts and Crafts in style, sources that address this style also may be of interest.

American Bungalow
P.O. Box 756
Sierra Madre, Calif. 91025-0756

Arts and Crafts Resource Directory
http://www.ragtime.org/ragtime

Craftsman Home Owners
Roycroft Associates
31 South Grove Street
East Aurora, N.Y. 14052

Gamble House Bookstore
4 Westmoreland Place
Pasadena, Calif. 91103

Greene and Greene Center
for the Study of the Arts and Crafts
Movement in America
Huntington Library
1151 Oxford Road
San Marino, Calif. 91108

Historic Preservation
National Trust
for Historic Preservation
1785 Massachusetts Avenue, N.W.
Washington, D.C. 20036

National Register of Historic Places
National Park Service
U.S. Department of the Interior
P.O. Box 37127
Washington, D.C. 20013-7127

National Trust
for Historic Preservation
1785 Massachusetts Avenue, N.W.
Washington, D.C. 20036

Old-House Interiors
Dovetale Publishers
2 Main Street
Gloucester, Mass. 01930

The Old-House Journal
Dovetale Publishers
2 Main Street
Gloucester, Mass. 01930

Preservation Assistance Division
National Park Service
U.S. Department of the Interior
P.O. Box 37127
Washington, D.C. 20013-7127

Tile Heritage Foundation
Box 1850
Healdsburg, Calif. 95448

FURTHER READING

PRIMARY SOURCES

From 1900 to 1930 hundreds of little books and pamphlets illustrated bungalow elevations and floor plans, which allowed would-be owners to write for more elaborate plans or even order prefabricated bungalows. Few libraries collect these, and they are hard to come by at secondhand bookstores. The best collection is at the Library of Congress. The most useful are the following:

Comstock, William Phillips, and Clarence Eaton Schermerhorn. *Bungalows, Camps and Mountain Houses.* New York: W. T. Comstock Company, 1908. 1915 edition reprinted with a new introduction by Tony P. Wrenn. Washington, D.C.: American Institute of Architects Press, 1990.

Useful and available. The 1924 edition is actually the best, because it includes much information on Antonin Necho-doma in Puerto Rico.

Keeler, Charles. *The Simple Home.* 1904. Reprint. Salt Lake City: Peregrine Smith, 1979.

A little book of advice on furniture and furnishings designed to make every bungalow a snug respite.

Murmann, Eugene O. *California Gardens.* Los Angeles: Eugene O. Murmann, 1914.

The title suggests regionalism, but the information and designs apply throughout the United States.

Saylor, Henry H. *Bungalows.* Philadelphia: John C. Winston Company, 1911.

Presents a good survey of the bungalow from foundation to sewage disposal.

Stickley, Gustav, ed. *Craftsman Bungalows: 59 Homes from "TheCraftsman."* 1903–16. Reprint. NewYork: Dover Publications, 1988.

Reproduces thirty-six articles from Stickley's magazine, complete with original illustrations and floor plans.

White, Charles E., Jr. *Bungalow Book.* New York: Macmillan, 1923.

Like Saylor, White (a Prairie School architect) tries to cover all aspects of the bungalow.

Wilson, Henry L. *The Bungalow Book.* Chicago: Henry L. Wilson, 1910.

Wilson ("the Bungalow Man") provides a good introduction through elevations and floor plans that give an idea of what the small contemporary bungalow books were like.

RECENT TITLES

King, Anthony D. *The Bungalow: TheProduction of a Global Culture.* London: Routledge and Kegan Paul, 1984.

As the subtitle indicates, the book explores the international ram-ifications of the bungalow's spread from continent to continent.

Lancaster, Clay. *The American Bungalow, 1880–1930.* New York: Abbeville Press, 1985.

_____. "The American Bungalow," *ArtBulletin* 40 (September 1958).

Lancaster's work, especially in the article, is the beginning of the revival of interest in the bungalow.

Robertson, Cheryl. "The Resort to theRustic: Simple Living and the California Bungalow." In Kenneth R. Trapp, et al. *The Arts and Crafts Movement in California: Living the Good Life.* Oakland Museum. NewYork: Abbeville Press, 1993.

A wide-ranging essay with fascinating footnotes that refer to a wealth of sources.

Winter, Robert. *The California Bungalow.* Los Angeles: Hennessey and Ingalls, 1980.

_____. "The Common American Bungalow." In Charles W. Moore, Kathryn Smith, and Peter Becker, eds. *Home Sweet Home: American Domestic Vernacular Architecture.* New York: Rizzoli, 1983.

The book was intended to sell the bungalow to its readers. The article was an attempt to compensate for the book's focus on the cream of the crop.

CREDITS

A practical and compact solution for storing books in small spaces was a revolving library stand. This Mission-style reproduction in oak or cherry is spindled and rotates 360 degrees. Courtesy L. and J. G. Stickley.

Alexander Vertikoff dedicates this book to Nora, Cole, and Carmen, whose love and patience provided the foundation for it.

Robert Winter and Alexander Vertikoff wish especially to thank the owners who invited us into their bungalows. Without them, the book would not have been able to present such a wonderful collection of American bungalows. Our thanks go to all of the following:

Marlene H. Bessel and Mitchell K. Baker, Ron Bernstein, Mr. and Mrs. Michael Borchardt, Jane Brackman and Rod Holcomb, Olivia Dresher, Jane S. and John A. Edginton, Donald and Meg Gertmenian, Allen Schnaiberg and Edith Harshbarger, Janet F. Jaeger, Eleanor H. Klein, the Reverend James Lawrence and Martha Lusk at the Swedenborgian Church, Betty and John Merritt, Maya Moran, Alison and Mitchell Prince, Diana Stuart and Ted Rabinowitsh, Miriam and Stuart Reisbord, Marnie Ross Schlitt, Jacob H. and Julitta M. Schmidt, Nancy E. Strathearn at Craftsman Farms, Alan and Laura Tanaka, Kathy and Phil Taylor, Jim and Marie Via, Arthur and Helen Vykouk, Holly Wahlberg, Mary F. Ward, and Kenneth Weikal.

We also are grateful for the invaluable advice and assistance of Tim Andersen, Edward Bosley, John Brinkmann, Robert Cangelosi, Paul Duchscherer, Charlie Fisher, Patricia Gay, David Gebhard, John Hildreth, Myrick Howard, Alan Johnson, Margery Krumwiede, Carla Lind, Kennon Miedema, Richard Mouck, Tom Owen, Pamela Post, Mary Rouse, Bruce and Yoshiko Smith, Kathy Holt Springston, Tim Turner, Sue Vec, Harriet von Bretton, and Dale Patrick Wolicki.

In Diane Maddex we had a great editor who offered many ideas, including the concept for the book itself. We also thank all the staff of Archetype Press for their assistance in helping us turn the words and photographs into a book. For her hours and hours at the word processor, Jean Viggiano deserves our appreciation.

All contemporary color photographs were taken by Alexander Vertikoff, except for views in the Bungalow Bazaar section and chapter openers furnished by manufacturers. Photographs by Robert Winter appear on page 32, left; page 35, left and center; page 36, right; and page 37, right. All historic illustrations come from the author's collection, except for the following: page 12, bottom (India Office, London); pages 14–15 (Robert Judson Clark); and pages 20–21 (Greene and Greene Library at the Huntington Library).

Robert Winter
Alexander Vertikoff

INDEX